Bisex

Bisexuality

Confessions of bisexual men and women

JASON DOUGLAS

SENATE

Bisexuality

Previously published in paperback in 1970 by
Canova Press Ltd, London

This paperback edition published in 1997 by Senate,
an imprint of Random House UK Ltd, Random House,
20 Vauxhall Bridge Road, London SW1V 2SA.

Copyright © Jason Douglas 1967

All rights reserved. This publication may not be reproduced,
stored in a retrieval system or transmitted, in any form or by any
means, electronic, mechanical, photocopying or otherwise, without
the prior written permission of the publishers.

ISBN 1 85958 503 5

Printed and bound in Great Britain by
Cox & Wyman, Reading, Berkshire

CONTENTS

1 The Nature of Bisexuality   7

2 The Making of a Bisexual   25

3 The All-round Lover   47

4 The Bisexual Woman   70

5 The Bisexual Man   93

6 The Nymphomaniac   115

7 The Satyr   131

8 The Bisexual in Literature   151

9 The Bisexual and the Future   178

CHAPTER 1: THE NATURE OF BISEXUALITY

All men and women are, to a certain extent, bisexual. This does not, however, imply that they are necessarily capable of deviated sexual behaviour. They are, to all intents and purposes, "normal" sexual beings, but the fact remains that they are bisexual. A great deal of controversy and confusion surrounds the term "bisexuality" and most of it springs from our certain knowledge that there are only two sexes, that "normal" sexual pairing requires the participation of one man and one woman and that any other combination of the sexes, *i.e.* man with man, woman with woman, is demonstrative of deviated behaviour.

This is, albeit true, a very simple way of looking at the question of sex and sexual expression, and it is perhaps held so widely because it is more convenient than accurate. For this view to have any real force, it must postulate that all men are totally masculine, and that all women are totally feminine. Just as most sophisticated societies prefer monogamy to polygamy for purely selfish, *i.e.* economical, social and moral reasons, so it is more convenient to divide human beings, from a sexual behavioural point of view, into normal and deviated categories. But the encouragement of monogamy does not eradicate the impulse to polygamy any more than the categories "normal" and "deviated" make a man or woman exclusively hetero- or homosexual. In other words, such a position would only be practically tenable if the majority of men and women belonged totally to their apparent sex and indulged in nothing but the accepted sexual activities of that sex. Clinically, however, it is held that no such "complete" human being exists.

A child's sex is decided at birth solely on the visual evidence of the genitals. Fortunately, in the vast majority of cases, this evidence is sufficient and accurate. But there are exceptions, as we shall see, and this decision cannot take into account the possibility that in later years the child may have a non-exclusive sexual urge, or, in other words, may be a bisexual. In this connection we should always remember that the sex determining factors are extremely small in number, and that both masculine and feminine elements are present in the foetus. In the early stages of its development, the foetus is sexless, or bisexual in the true sense of the word, *i.e.* belonging to both sexes. By this we mean that the potential to be either masculine or feminine exists and that the foetus has no truly determinable sex. In the later stages of gestation, however, one set of determining factors, either the masculine or the feminine, are developed more strongly than the other, with the result that in the normal, healthy baby a penis or a vagina is developed, and thus the sex of the child is determined. But the other undeveloped genes and chromosomes, *i.e.* those of the opposite sex, are *not* destroyed, nor do they mysteriously and conveniently vanish. They are present in the new born baby and remain so throughout life. Thus when we describe someone as a "real man" or a very "feminine woman" we are commenting upon their determined sex, and their apparent behaviour. These are the normal people, the sexually balanced who seem to be truly and completely of one sex. But we cannot know this from such evidence. The best we can say is that they are *primarily* masculine or feminine. The opposite sex, to put it another way, is merely unobtrusive in their appearance and behaviour, but it is certainly present.

Bisexuality is the word used to describe a situation whereby a person is known to be both male and female, to belong to both sexes. Thus, as we have seen, from a clinical point of view, all people can be described as bisexual. This usage, however, implies no more than an acknowledgement that factors of the opposite sex exist within the normal man and woman. Such usage does not imply any description of their sexual proclivities or behaviour. Extreme cases of bisexuality are commonly given other names. For example, the man who, though physically masculine, feels himself mentally to be a woman, and seeks to express this feeling by dressing in feminine clothing is called a transvestite. The transexual is a person who actively desires to be a woman, a man who possesses a conviction that Nature has made some error. Frequently such cases possess a distinctly feminine, or, if they are women, distinctly, masculine bodies. However, these convictions are very definite evidence of bisexuality since the individual belongs to both sexes either by having a masculine mind in a female body or *vice versa*. Contrary to majority belief, however, such people are not necessarily homosexual. There is simply a dichotomy between their apparent sex and their own beliefs about their sex.

Somewhere between the extremes of normal, balanced bisexuality and transvestism and transexuality lie the people, also designated simply bisexual, who are our main concern. It is becoming increasingly common for the word "bisexual" to be used exclusively to describe those who enjoy and even actively seek sexual relations with members of both their own and the opposite sex. They are, in other words, men and women who, despite the ability to lead a normal heterosexual life also indulge in homosexual and lesbian practices. Such people have a propensity for homosexual liaisons, which is equally matched by their propensity for heterosexual activity. Because of this it is inaccurate to regard them as homosexuals. They are simply bisexuals who enjoy the favours of men and women virtually indiscriminately.

In the heterosexual individual one sex has been successfully developed and the elements of the opposite sex which still exist within them are dormant. As a result, their libido is directed primarily towards the opposite sex. However, as Kinsey overwhelmingly proved, very few people indeed do not have some homosexual experiences, often quite apart from those which naturally occur in adolescence when a youth or girl is virtually experimenting in search of his or her correct, satisfying sexual role. Such acts very often have little lasting significance, but they may be taken as evidence of bisexuality. It is a demonstration of the opposite sex's presence in the individual. Often it is fleeting and isolated, and its importance is a negative one. It confirms the heterosexuality of the individual, and not his or her homosexuality.

The bisexual, on the other hand, has not sufficiently stressed one sex in his psychological development. In the case of man, while it is true that the masculine genes and chromosomes have been developed, it is also true that the feminine ones have more or less kept pace. Such a person is marginally male, *i.e.* he possesses a male body, male genitals, but he has definite feminine traits because the female elements in his make-up have not lain dormant. The same position applies to the bisexual woman.

When we say, however, that such people possess masculine or feminine traits, we do not mean that they are recognisably lesbian or effeminate. The woman who dresses and acts as much like a man as possible is almost certain to be an exclusive lesbian. The effeminate male will either be homosexual or transvestite. The true bisexual is not, in this sense, recognisable. The bisexual woman is likely to be womanly, even overtly feminine. The masculine elements in her nature will be apparent in her strength of intellect, an almost masculine energy, and an extrovert, non-maternal approach to life. The bisexual male is quite likely to be a good athlete, to be absorbed by masculine pursuits, but the feminine elements of his nature will reveal themselves in an increased sensibility and sensitivity, a gentleness and perception which is more properly regarded as feminine. The result is what is frequently known as the artistic or creative temperament. The combination of strength and sensivity often predisposes such people to artistic endeavour.

One of the most crucial aspects of bisexuality is its current interest value. As we have already suggested, the use of the term almost exclusively to describe people who enjoy sexual relations with both sexes is a fairly recent phenomenon. This interest and usage of the term is extremely relevant, for it has already been suggested that bisexuality is the most popular contemporary vice, and the reasons for this go some way to indicate the nature of the condition itself.

There have always been bisexuals. The idea that it is a totally new state is quite erroneous. It is as old as the human race, and many well-known historical figures have been avowed bisexuals. Why then does the condition seem so suddenly prevalent and widespread? There are three main reasons: the increased tolerance of the contemporary moral climate; the acceptance of the fact that sexual pleasure should be as wide and various as possible within the context of the individual's wishes; and the recent reappraisal of social attitudes to homosexuality.

It is important to remember that the bisexual of the past was subject to very great social and moral pressures and that his knowledge of sexology and psychology was dramatically scant. Homosexuality was condemned by virtually all societies, and the bisexual's impulse towards his or her own sex would be indistinguishable from out-and-out homosexuality. Thus only those placed outside the range of social condemnation by power and position could really afford to indulge their sexual natures to the full. Today psychological and sexological research has shown us that sex is not a source of shame. We have been taught to accept and constructively utilise the gift of sex. This, combined with the growh of a permissive moral climate has lessened if not removed the pressure to conform sexually. Now it is possible to conform, within certain limits, solely to one's own impulse, rather than to the abstract dictates of society.

The bisexual woman, of course, has always enjoyed a greater degree of freedom because lesbianism has never been so forcibly repressed and punished as male homosexuality. No legal pressures have been brought to bear on women and in recent years the subject has lost much of its aura of shame. Similarly, attitudes towards homosexuality are becoming increasingly lenient. Even in countries where this leniency has not yet extended to legal embodiment, the social attitude has become more tolerant. Thus bisexual men feel less inhibited in expressing the homosexual side of their natures.

Permissiveness itself has done much to create a climate in which bisexuality can flourish. It is widely accepted now that people are curious about sex and this allows the bisexual to explore his own nature to a much greater degree. The old beliefs about the sanctity and sexual exclusiveness of marriage have been severely attacked, and the much publicised practice of wife-swapping is one which creates an almost ideal situation for the bisexual. Wife-swapping orgy situations automatically sweep away ingrained inhibitions. Participants take courage from their companions and the fear of criticism is allayed. In this way the bisexual finds an ideal situation to exercise his sexual potential to the full. Similarly phenomena such as swap clubs and personal advertising have brought the bisexual out into the open. When a married couple advertise, as they frequently do today, for a single partner, male or female, it is obvious that bisexual behaviour will be accepted, is, in fact, being actively sought. The man or girl who offers to join a married couple in sexual acts knows that he or she will be involved in some homosexual activities. These phenomena have given the bisexual a powerful confidence he has without doubt hitherto lacked.

It is, in many ways, difficult not to agree with the bisexual who habitually maintains that he is a sexually privileged creature thanks to his natural ability to enjoy the best of both worlds. Strictly speaking this attitude is a reasonable one, for it is quite wrong to regard the bisexual as a deviate, or his behaviour as evidence of perversion. The bisexual does not seek to be "cured" for there is neither means or need to "cure" him. The bisexual personality is only in need of help when for some reason, he is unable to accept his dual sexual interest. In this sense he should perhaps more properly be regarded as a sexual phenomenon, and not material for a clinical study. However, as we shall see, the view that he automatically enjoys the best of both worlds is a facile and often unfounded one. The roots of bisexuality, its causes, are often evidence of genuine psychological disturbance.

What is particularly interesting, from the clinical point of view, is the unusually powerful sexual urge which is common to many bisexuals. Their desire is often unusually great and it is tempting to see in their catholicity of sexual taste an attempt on Nature's part to satisfy this exaggerated sexual urge. For this reason, many bisexuals suffer from satyriasis or nymphomania. Their sexual drive is so great that they are continually seeking a degree of sexual fulfilment which constantly eludes them. More often than not this fulfilment is of an emotional and spiritual nature. Such people are generally expert sexual practitioners who achieve physical satisfaction easily, but this happy state of affairs is not infrequently accompanied by an emotional frigidity which drives them fruitlessly and exhaustingly from bed to bed. This constant emotional frustration can easily result in more serious mental disturbances of one kind or another. However, the cause of the trouble is not properly their bisexuality, but their endless quest and inevitable failure.

It is, therefore, wiser to regard the bisexual as a social and sexual phenomenon, and to examine his motives and impulses through the evidence of his behaviour. What sort of person is the bisexual? There is no easy answer to this question, for bisexual personalities are as varied as those of any other group of human beings. The common traits which may safely be elucidated do not clarify the personality type to any great extent. The male bisexual is likely to be cultured and artistically inclined. He will have an unusual sensitivity, a powerful sexual urge and a frank interest in all aspects of sex. The female bisexual is generally tough-minded, clear-headed and passionate. She will be outspoken and will seek sexual satisfaction without embarrassment or hesitation. She will, in all probability, consider herself the equal of men and, unlike most women, will not be particularly maternal, and will enjoy the company of other like-minded women as much as that of men. But within these broad character delineations, the bisexual man and woman are as contradictory and surprising as any human being. They may be frankly physical in their sexual approach, or passionately romantic. They may be stable and docile, or erratic and volatile. The one thing we may be absolutely certain of is that they will seek a variety of sexual experiences and be possessed of a powerful, demanding libido. All these points are clearly demonstrated by the statements of bisexuals themselves.

"When you boil it all down, all that can be said about my sex life is that both men and women turn me on. I don't think in terms of different sexes, but react entirely to individuals. This week it may be a boy, next week a girl. I tend to form intense but short-lived relationships with people, and these relationships invariably include some sort of sexual expression. But there is nothing deliberate about it. It just seems to happen, and I never deliberately consider the sex of my lover at the time. Of course, there is a definite difference in the quality of the emotional and mental response to the different sexes, but I cannot honestly say that this is a matter for consideration, or that I am aware of any particular difference in sexual activity. I always play the active role in my affairs with men, so really there is very little contrast."

This statement by a man of thirty reveals what might be regarded as the basic bisexual temperament. It is particularly interesting to note that the emotional element in his relationships is extremely unstable. He declares that he has never really been in love, but has often thought that he was. His relationships are, as a result, intense but short-lived. Clinically we would say that this man is emotionally unfulfilled. He changes partners so quickly because he expects and demands too much, too soon. He is not content, or perhaps not even able, to let a relationship grow and mature at a natural pace. He places sex first, cannot really conceive of a meaningful relationship without some sexual activity. But he tires quickly, and moves on. His symptoms are, in a sense, very close to those displayed by the genuine satyr, but his search is not compulsive or frenzied. He simply drifts from person to person, from sex to sex without any real effort. For this reason he is not a true satyr. This, plus his insistence that he is not aware of any significant difference between the two sexes from the point of view of sexual relations with them, marks him out as a true bisexual. It is important to note that this man does not react indiscriminately to the sexes. All men and women are not attractive. He exercises choice, just as the heterosexual man and woman do. The only difference is that his potential for choice is greater since individual members of both sexes appeal to him.

In direct contrast is this statement by a divorced woman of thirty-seven.

"For years I refused to regard myself as bisexual. I was a normal, heterosexual woman as far as I was concerned. But then I had a lesbian experience, my marriage broke up and I was forced to take stock of myself and my situation. I now see that I am bisexual, but I don't regard this as a blessing. I know that many people do, but not me.

"I am virtually frigid with men. That's my trouble, but it doesn't mean that I am an out and out lesbian. I just don't find real physical satisfaction with a man. I am not mentally frigid. On the contrary, I am very excited by men and want to have successful sex with them. But it never compares physically with the pleasure I get from another woman.

"To put it in a nutshell, I need men emotionally and women sexually. Or at least that's how it seems to have worked out. I enjoy, even revel in the sensation of being a woman, cared for and protected by a strong, tender man. Emotionally, that is the only possible situation as far as I am concerned. But sexually nothing much happens. On the other hand, a woman can bring me remarkably intense pleasure, but I can't form a lasting or satisfactory emotional relationship with her. Women just don't appeal that way at all, and if they try to be substitute men, I'm completely put off. I can't bear 'butch' lesbians. I like women to be women and men to be men, even though its selfish, I suppose, that I demand this and yet move so freely myself between the two."

This woman's problem is not nearly as isolated as it may at first seem. Many women tend to be bisexual by necessity, the root of the problem being largely physical. Women differ from men not only in that they are capable of multiple orgasm, but in the very quality of the orgasm itself. Many women do not experience vaginal orgasm at all. Still more experience it, but find that it does not compare favourably with the clitoridean orgasm. One woman significantly described the difference as that between a momentous flash (via the clitoris) and an attentuated rolling (via the vagina). It seems, from what she says, that the woman quoted above is incapable of vaginal orgasm and that she has been continually frustrated by her male lover's lack of knowledgeability. Of course, it is quite possible that she has a particularly small or hidden clitoris which her male partners have failed to locate. A woman, simply because she has a much better comprehension of female needs, would not overlook the clitoris. The woman concerned in all probability does not encourage manual or oral sex when she is with a man simply because it recalls her lesbian habits, and because of her emotional need to be dominated and possessed, symbolised by the reception of the penis. However, all the evidence points to the fact that she could lead a perfectly satisfactory heterosexual life if she found the right partner.

But a great many women do not, and bisexuality is an apparent answer to this problem. This woman is not, however, unnaturally bisexual. Her bisexuality may well be prompted by necessity, but she obviously has no aversion to lesbianism. Physically, lesbian acts are enjoyable, but her emotional impulse is entirely towards the male sex. This point in underlined by her avowed aversion to "butch" lesbians, *i.e.* to lesbians who seek to emulate men. This is a very common aversion among bisexuals. To refer back to our first statement, in discussing his homosexual liaisons, the man said:

"I can't bear effeminate men. I do, of course, go with exclusively homosexual men, but never with limp-wristed, lisping pseudo-women. They have to be manly. To look and behave like men. When I am with a male lover, I want to enjoy a male body, a masculine mind."

True bisexuals are usually insistent upon this point. It is logical that they should reject the pseudo-male or pseudo-female, for their concern is with both sexes and with recognisable members of whichever sex it may be. If a man insists that his male partner should be an imitation woman, it is usually because he is seeking to repress his homosexuality, to clothe its practice, at least symbolically, in the illusion of heterosexuality. The same is true of the woman who seeks an active, aggressive lesbian "man". The bisexual seldom experiences a comparable shame or fear. The taint of homosexuality is, as far as he is concerned, expunged by his heterosexual relationships, and the same applies to the bisexual woman, although here the problem is less acute simply because lesbianism is generally held to be more innocuous than male homosexuality. But to return to our main point, most bisexuals are in agreement that there would be no point in bisexuality if their partners were chosen from the ranks of imitation men and women. The bisexual has a frank and, to most intents and purposes, a natural response to both sexes. He or she has no wish to confuse the sexes, but to enjoy each in their separate individual ways.

In this respect, not all bisexuals follow the pattern of our two witnesses quoted above. Some men are intensely aware of the differences in having sexual relations with men and women, much like the divorced woman already referred to. Some women, on the other hand, seek to play an active role in their bisexual lesbian relationships, just as a small but significant number of men elect to play the passive role in their bisexual homosexual activities.

James W, a university graduate in his late twenties, said:

"I have absolutely no doubt about the sexual differences of my partners. To me, this is the essence of bisexuality. In a sense I regard the heterosexual part of my life as the natural one. There is something which I cannot define about being in bed with a woman which feels right and natural. I have no doubt that I shall get married and probably have children. I feel that I need that sort of emotional and social security. Sex with a woman is inevitably bound-up with settling down and raising a family, with building a home and leading a reasonably conventional existence. But although I always feel this, and am certain that this is how my life will eventually go, I do not envisage that I will be able to leave boys alone.

"Part of my homosexual interest is certainly based on the feeling of not yet wanting to get settled down. You see, I tend to have long-term relationships with women — I have a regular girl friend at the moment — but very brief casual relationships with boys. Somehow this impermanence gives me an important illusion of freedom, even though I know that I am only deferring the inevitable.

"But there is more to it than that. The forbidden nature of homosexuality attracts me too. It is somehow adventurous, and that, I think, is very important to me. And I feel less responsibility in homosexual relationships. With a girl, you can't be casual when sex is involved. Sex means so much more to a woman, it is so closely involved with birth and homes and things. A man has a definite responsibility towards a girl. He has to make her feel safe and wanted, has to care for her in all senses of the word. But a man so often feels a completely physical need. He does not always want to be considering another person's complex needs and fears. He just wants sex. Other men understand this. The whole thing is much less demanding. And because I am a very strongly sexed person I'm sure that even after marriage I shall need sexual variety and I shall seek it with boys."

This unusually lucid account of bisexual attitudes contains a great many truths about bisexuality in general, its causes and effects. Like many other men, James W's impulse is not equally balanced to both sexes. He is, for want of a better description, primarily heterosexual. This attitude is very largely the result of his background and of conditioning. He is truly bisexual, in so far as both sexes attract him strongly, but he has deliberately separated the two forms of sexuality. Women are almost objects of veneration to him. He has been taught that women are "special" creatures who need certain cares and reassurances from men. These he is prepared to give, but the demand conflicts with a purely physical need which he satisfies with men. His care of women is probably exaggerated. He is sensitive towards them, and is concerned to behave well. He does not, to coin a phrase, believe in trifling with their affections. Men, or rather boys, for he always deliberately chooses male partners much younger than himself, do not require, in his opinion, this special concern. He simply takes his pleasure on the assumption that all men are like him and expect no emotional involvement.

It is obvious from all this that James W's background is a very conventional one, and that he is very considerably motivated by received attitudes. Hence when he speaks of homosexuality as being "adventurous" and "forbidden" we may see strong evidence of a revolt against his accepted background. Closely interwoven with this is his sense of freedom within homosexual relationships. Freedom, of course, is frequently confused with rebellion and is yet another aspect of his protest against conforming to a "reasonably conventional existence".

These are very common feelings among bisexuals. Very often one aspect of their dual sexual expression is stressed because of educational and environmental pressures, while the other aspect becomes a symbol of rebellion or dissatisfaction. James W's is a very clearly defined case, but his feelings are shared by a great many bisexuals for a variety of reasons.

Moira R is a model wife, good homemaker and mother, and has a frank enjoyment of sex with her husband. However, she is also bisexual and has had, for a number of years, a series of discreet lesbian relationships. Like James W she insists that the two aspects of her sex life are quite different.

"If a woman makes my sort of marriage safe, conventional, unadventurous, she is bound to get a bit frustrated. Or at least I think so. My marriage is marvellous. I really have no complaints, but sexually it is confining. My husband has very set ideas about sex, about the roles of men and women, and so our sex life, although good and frequent, is pretty classic. By that I mean that there is no room for variation. I am expected to be the passive woman. I am expected to receive pleasure, to have children. And that is about it. That's perfectly satisfactory, of course, I know hundreds of women would be delighted to be assured of so much. I know it is wrong of me to want more. But there it is.

"I am, I suppose, active by nature. I love giving pleasure and although I know that by lying on my back I do give my husband pleasure, it's not very definite, is it? With my women friends I always play an active role. I really don't care if they never touch me. I just enjoy giving them pleasure, to see them getting real satisfaction from me. In a way it is selfish because I enjoy it so much, but there's plenty in it for them, too."

Moira R has never taken a male lover, nor will she seriously consider the idea. Like many women, she has a strong masculine streak in her personality and seeks to be the dominant partner in some sexual situations. Her husband, however, cannot or will not accept this and she turns to women who are much younger than herself. There is undoubtedly an element of power-seeking in these activities. She chooses young women because her age and experience give her more power over them than she could ever hope to gain over any but the most submissive man. In typical bisexual fashion, such men do not at all appeal to her.

Her bisexuality is also indicative of revolt. Although she accepts and has made a success of a very conventional marriage, a very placid and ordinary life, she has had to make a conscious effort so to do. In her lesbian relationships, Moira R is expressing a repressed impatience with her life. To take a male lover, we might suggest, would be to conform to the pattern. But lesbianism successfully symbolises her basic irritation with convention, as well as satisfying her lust for a more active and powerful sexual role.

There is little evidence of rebellion, however, in the behaviour of Peter K, although his case may well at first suggest this. In fact, he has little to revolt against and his sexual activities should be regarded as evidence of his need for different sensations from different sexes. He is an extremely handsome, slightly built young man who is engaged to a small, very feminine, rather passive girl. He always seeks such women, and finds any but the most overtly soft and feminine girls quite unattractive. At the same time he is deeply attracted to well-built older men, with whom he plays a passive sexual role. Once again, no other sort of men attract him.

Peter K's sex life is very closely concerned with the adoption of roles. He is a demanding, harsh heterosexual lover, and a passive, acquiescent homosexual one. With his fiancée he likes to present himself as a brutal, ultra-masculine male, but with a man he seeks to be treated much as he treats his own girl-friend. When he is with the girl, he admits that he imagines himself as one of his muscular, demanding male lovers, but when he is actually with one of these men, he identifies with his fiancée. This, he claims, makes him a better lover, for he has a greater understanding of women's sensations. In fact, this behaviour is more obviously suggestive of pronounced homosexual fear. In each situation he seeks, by imagination, to achieve a semblance of heterosexuality.

As a boy, his pronounced good looks and slight physique caused him to be often taken for a homosexual. He began to envy men of a markedly masculine, *i.e.* different, physical type. Consequently, this envy grow into identification with them which in turn caused him to seek out passively feminine women with whom he could enact an exaggeratedly masculine role. Naturally, for homosexual practices he chose men of a similar physical type, but always wanted to be a "woman" with them.

In fact, his whole sexual behaviour pattern suggests that he is considerably more strongly homosexual than heterosexual. However, probably because of his boyhood experiences, he wishes to be acknowledged as a definite, indisputably heterosexual man. He is, however, truly bisexual in that he is attracted by both sexes and performs satisfactorily with both. But he is so concerned with the impression he makes, with the role he elects to play that he does not enjoy any deep emotional relationship with any of his partners. His fiancée appeals to him primarily because of the opportunity she provides for him to indulge in his masculine role, whereas he is always careful to maintain a very casual relationship with his male partners, thus precluding any possibility of a deeper attachment. This strongly suggests that he would be happier in an exclusively homosexual situation, but he has opted for this peculiarly ambivalent form of bisexuality which is quite common among men of this kind.

Thus we see that the bisexual personality differs radically in its motives and attitudes. We can only repeat that the bisexual has a stronger than usual sexual urge and, in many, many cases, finds it extremely difficult to form a deep, lasting and tenable emotional bond with one person. Because of the catholicity of his or her tastes, the bisexual is often made the object of envy. The uninformed tend to view them as uninhibited sexual athletes who occupy a world of limitless opportunity. This is, however, a short sighted view, applicable only to a small, fortunate percentage. For the majority, their sexual dualism is an alternative to other unfulfilled needs. Very few bisexuals can balance the demands of their disparate sexual natures. Most are fundamentally lonely, seeking the apparently unobtainable with only the poor compensation of fleeting sexual pleasure. Even those, like Moira R, who do manage to maintain some permanent, steady emotional relationship are not fundamentally satisfied and are always afraid that their other sexual activities constitute a threat to the little permanence they have.

Bisexuality is, then at best a mixed blessing. It is a sexual condition which, although by no means as serious or stultifying as some aberrations and perversions, almost inevitably cloaks some psychological wound or maldevelopment and which all too frequently acts as a barrier to true happiness and fulfilment.

CHAPTER 2: THE MAKING OF A BISEXUAL

It should be obvious at once that the mere fact that the genes and chromosomes of the opposite sex develop alongside those of an individual's "true" sex is not sufficient to explain fully the bisexual's behaviour. The fact that a shadow of the opposite sex exists within a particular man or woman does not automatically mean that they indulge in homosexual or lesbian as well as heterosexual practices. The potential for homosexual behaviour exists in a great many people, but it is not expressed. To a certain extent it would be correct to say that this tendency is repressed, although it is very often an automatic process, almost a reflex action, prompted by belief and educational pressures. It is sometimes quite erroneously believed that the only safeguard against homosexual temptation is to be disgusted by or indifferent to the idea of such practices. This is not true. Many people are aware of a distinct attraction to individual members of their own sex, but they do not give way to this attraction for various reasons. Occasionally the attraction is acknowledged, but any sexual expression is strictly forbidden by the person who experiences this attraction. We see this often in relationships whereby older men or women befriend and help a younger member of their own sex. Such couples often enjoy a very deep mutual affection which is, at least in the case of the one partner, based on sexual attraction but who deliberately subjugates this feeling in a normal friendship.

Further, the bisexual impulse often exists in people without their having any thought of giving it a sexual expression. Indeed, such an idea would horrify them. The explanation for this is quite simple, and does not imply either a superhuman willpower or a disturbing degree of auto-suppression. Such people tend to have rather weak sexual urges and, provided they are not totally frustrated, are usually in a position of sexual satisfaction which removes any sexual impulse from their relationship with members of their own sex. These relationships, intense and often generous, are, however, based on a bisexual impulse, but are entirely asexual in conduct and motive.

The true bisexual, however, as we know, is very much aware of his dual sexual impulse and is concerned to express it fully. In short, the expression of bisexual tendencies in the form of sexual acts with both men and women is not a necessary outcome of bisexuality. In fact, practising bisexuals have to learn and develop their sexual propensities just as a heterosexual person does. Because of this it is tempting to assume that the first voluntarily sought sexual experience of the bisexual is an indication of his or her primary sex, *e.g.* if a girl's first experience is with a man, we may assume that she is predominantly heterosexual. However, this is not a safe yardstick, and no coherent definitive pattern emerges from the subsequent behaviour of bisexuals which would indicate that their first experiences are particularly revealing. The young bisexual is open to the same influences and pressures as heterosexual individuals, and are equally susceptible to accompanying circumstances and impressions. Thus it is quite possible for their dual sexual urge to be awakened by an unfortunate or unpleasant first experience.

Indeed, the available evidence suggests that we should regard the awareness of bisexuality as an awakening of the second sex within the individual. Adolescents and young people are too concerned with the whole mystery of sex, for the most part, to consider in great detail the direction of their sexual impulses. Most young people, including bisexuals, are aware of what is considered normal, *i.e.* that a boy's sexual impulse is directed towards a girl, and *vice versa*, and we should not underestimate the importance of this conditioning in the selection of first sexual partners. However, there are cases where the selection is "blind", where the individual simply follows his or her instinct to satisfy an over-riding curiosity about sex and its expression.

The important point to remember is that early, or youthful experiences often have far reaching consequences for the later sexual development of the adolescent. Just as the first conscious experience of orgasm, or even of sexual arousal, is almost certain to be revealing of the mature behaviour of the fetishist or the exclusive homosexual, so the first shared sexual experience of the bisexual often sets up ripples whose effects are not fully appreciated until much later in life. In the next chapter we shall see that a great many bisexuals do not discover their full nature until they are quite old and fully experienced sexually. However, for the moment we are concerned with the earlier discovery of bisexuality, with, in general, people who discovered and recognised their full potential without the aid of such uninhibiting situations as wife-swapping or swap clubs to aid them. And it is this awareness which is crucial to the bisexual, not only because of the important and obvious influence it has upon his or her sex life, but because its discovery is the very thing which sets them apart from the exclusively heterosexual and homosexual. And from an objective point of view, the circumstances of the discovery often reveal the flaws in the personality for which bisexual expression is used as a substitute or to fill a scarcely acknowledged gap.

As we have already said, the range of bisexual experience is wide, and to search for one basic pattern is generally fruitless. For this reason, it should be borne in mind that the following testimonies and the conclusions drawn from them have been selected because they are indicative of various forms of behaviour and experiences which tend to be common to groups of bisexuals, although each statement may be radically different. This contrast serves to stress the disparate nature of the bisexual and his behaviour, but no single case is isolated, or remarkably unusual.

James W, for example, whose bisexual attitudes and motives were discussed in Chapter 1, relates a classic case of bisexual discovery.

"My first shared sexual experiences occurred at school. I attended a decent prep school and then moved on to a very highly rated public school. It was there that I learned about sex, although I in fact learned very little. Contrary to popular belief, all public schools are not hot beds of vice, although there is, obviously, always a degree of homosexuality. What else can one expect when you shut a lot of boys up together for weeks on end just when they are beginning to make discoveries about their own bodies and to develop a curiosity about sex? But generally homosexuality goes in waves in public schools. Up until I was about fifteen, there was very little. And then a group of seniors started a major movement.

"I didn't particularly enjoy it, curiously enough. One had very little choice in the matter, however, and, in any case, everybody did it. A school such as mine takes its tone and attitude from the senior common room, whether those attitudes be good or bad. And so one did not question the sexual behaviour to which one was exposed. One knew that this or that boy had been chosen and to have complained when your turn came would have been unthinkably bad form.

"But I must stress that we only had the haziest idea about the so-called rights and wrongs of the matter. As far as one could gather from the School Chaplain and similar worthies, *anything* to do with the genitals was *per se* wrong. There was absolutely no distinction between homosexuality and heterosexuality. That was far too sophisticated. One simply accepted the *status quo*. Most boys were glad of it, I think, because the alternative was miserable old masturbation.

"By the time I became a member of the Senior Common Room, the whole thing was pretty much accepted and I took a quite different attitude. My age and status meant that I could take the initiative, I could play the active role and I found that much more to my taste. I became very active indeed, even insatiable. My contemporaries, I think, with one exception, regarded the whole thing as a bit of a lark, but for me, my sexual affairs were the only thing that really made school bearable in the last three years.

"The extraordinary thing was that one never questioned what one was doing, even when one began to take a specific sexual interest in girls. You see, homosexuality was something that happened at school. One left all that behind the moment one went home, and then, being in one's teens, one was naturally exposed to girls and saw them, quite instinctively in my case, as potential sexual partners.

"As always happens, there was a wave of reaction at school against homosexuality. One or two of the fellows had actually had a girl during the vacs, and they returned with all sorts of theories about the evils of homosexuality, etc. Those of us who really enjoyed it were made to think a bit. Spoiling young lads' lives, and all that. But we weren't really equipped to defend our position and virtually overnight homosexuality was 'out', and endless imaginative speculations about girls was 'in'. I was still a heterosexual non-starter, but very much aware that girls were one's sexual goal. But I continued with my homosexual adventures, although they were necessarily less frequent and more furtive. I still hadn't made any decision, you understand, and only imperfectly understood the implications of bisexuality. It was simply a case of doing one thing at school and another at home.

"When I left school and went to the University, of course, I was too immersed in the newness of it all to think about sex very much. There were girls that we could meet on equal terms, and I soon got myself a girl friend. My first heterosexual experiences occurred at the University, and I can't recall that I felt anything special. I mean it was marvellous, exciting and all that, but no more than the usual elation young men feel at their first sexual success. I certainly didn't connect it in any way with my homosexual experiences. I never gave them a thought.

"And then, in my third year, I'd broken off with my girl, and none of the girls I was taking out at the time meant anything special, and I never tried to have intercourse with them. I imagine one or two would have let me, but I never could have casual sex with a girl. Sex follows naturally from an emotional involvement and, well, there just wasn't that sort of involvement.

"And then I became strongly attracted to a young first year boy. He was very slight and very pretty, little more than a boy really, and I found him physically irresistible. I think he was completely queer, but I don't really know. I never kept in touch with him after I came down. Anyway, I had him and thoroughly enjoyed it. It was then that I realised that I was bisexual, for after that I still wanted girls, reacted strongly to them, but I only had to see this boy semi-naked to want him violently.

"After a brief but acute crisis of conscience, I saw that nothing had changed. I began to have other boys in the town, — he was the only one at the University — and continued to go out with girls. That is more or less how it's been ever since. Boys briefly, occasionally, and girls when I feel some definite emotional bond with them. I have had about half a dozen affairs with girls, but I couldn't begin to count the number of boys I've had in my time."

A great many people believe that boarding schools are almost inevitably a breeding ground for homosexuals, but this is an exaggerated view. Although homosexual activities certainly occur there, little lasting damage is done simply because the situation is instinctively known to be false by the youths and children involved. James W clearly indicates the difference between home and school, and it is entirely logical that the habits and practices which are accepted unquestioningly in one environment should not be carried over into the other. For this reason, schoolboy homosexuality does not preclude normal heterosexual reactions and attractions. The moment the opportunity is created, Nature takes its course. It is much more likely, however, that the false environment of the boarding school should create an awakening of the bisexual impulse, and indeed many bisexuals do trace the roots or their homosexual awareness to such incidents.

Most children, if they learn about homosexuality at all, learn from the very start that it is wrong and prohibited. But in the exclusively male or female environment of a boarding school, as James W clearly points out, the prevailing code of behaviour is dictated by the fads and fancies of senior boys. There are, in fact, two codes, the official one, laid down by masters and governors, and a sort of underground one, dictated by the boys themselves. This latter is, naturally, more powerful because it implies status and conformity as well as a token revolution against the established order. Thus, in such a situation, homosexuality is not obviously or necessarily wrong. All sex is officially forbidden, or worse, simply not mentioned, so that homosexual practices are lumped together with masturbation and speculation about the opposite sex. Within the context of this false and enclosed society, homosexuality is "normal", an unremarkable fact of school life.

This does not mean, however, that all boys who pass through such institutions and gain experience of homosexuality are able to view the subject with equanimity in later life. For the majority, homosexual practices are relegated to childhood. In the wide world, they pursue a heterosexual path, and their impulses are quite firmly fixed on the opposite sex. But the truly bisexual, like James W, when they discover that the attraction for their own sex persists after schooldays are over, can cope more easily than those who have been completely protected from homosexuality and taught that it is wrong. In a sense, the bisexual has to accept the duality of his sexual impulse if he is to live comfortably with himself, and the man who, as a boy, has been exposed to homosexuality in an acceptable context, such as boarding school, does not have to surmount the barriers of prohibition, the sense of sin, which normally attends the discovery of the individual's deviated propensities. Once he has learned that his homosexuality does not exclude his being sexually aroused and fulfilled by girls, it is comparatively easy for him to reconcile the two aspects of his nature.

To return to James W himself, we recognise from all that he says that he is fundamentally immature. For all that his attitude to women is presented lucidly as mature and well-formed, almost the epitome of his class and background, there is constantly evidence of a contrary pull in his instincts. To put it bluntly, he equates women and his relationships with them with conformity. A relationship with a woman has one logical end — marriage and settling down. Yet he resists this. For all his insistence that he is incapable of having a sexual relationship with a girl unless he feels himself to be in love with her, it is obvious that none of his affairs have been based on any firm emotional bond. Obviously he fears conformity as symbolised by marriage and its responsibilities, and we may assume that he has broken off with his various girl friends for this reason. Under the pretence of looking for the right girl, he successfully avoids the responsibilities he regards as inevitable. His postponement is symptomatic of his fear, and it seems likely that his fear is based on the dual nature of his sexual impulse.

His flight into homosexuality, although convincingly presented as the fulfilling of a simple sexual need, is also evidence of immaturity. In these brief relationships, James W is recreating the circumstances of his childhood. The sex he has is uncomplicated, irresponsible, satisfying and entails no permanent relationship, has no definite preconceived goal. All this is in direct contrast to a relationship with a girl. In this connection it is significant that his male partners are always younger than himself. He favours teenagers, youths who are scarcely more than boys. This enables him to play a dominant role, but his superiority is false since the participants are unequally matched. With girls, of course, his sex and the accepted sexual role of the male naturally places him in a apparently superior position, but subconsciously James W doubts his ability to maintain this role, is by no means certain that he can successfully shoulder the full responsibilities of a husband, father and provider. In his relationships with young men, he symbolically returns to the irresponsible undemanding world of his childhood, and this sense of freedom is strengthened by his belief that his male partners expect nothing more than casual sexual pleasure from him.

This fundamental and dangerous immaturity is based undoubtedly on the fact that he has not, contrary to his statements and probably beliefs, succeeded in reconciling himself to his bisexual nature. Possessed of a strong, demanding sexual urge, he reacts quickly and powerfully to members of both sexes, but basically he does not know which he prefers. Prompted by received attitudes about the way one should live, and particularly about the male's responsibility towards women, he has added to the dilemma by separating the two forms of sexual expression and pleasure so radically. Ideally, James W should not marry, but his social position and background place a pressure on him to do so. In the world he is equipped to inhabit, a presentable wife is virtually essential. But he hangs back, passing through a series of pretended love situations and always withdrawing at the last moment. At such times, his homosexuality seems both a blessed relief and the curse which dogs his life and threatens any "lasting" relationship he might form. Caught in this dilemma, he avoids any deep emotional commitment and suffers from a sense of failure which is made worse by his refusing to acknowledge it. As a result, he fails to progress and mature emotionally.

The bisexual frequently suffers from such immaturity. Very often, he or she simply do not know what they want. The discovery of their potential for homosexual relationships is often shocking and painful, but is overcome or rendered neutral by their heterosexual urge. The dichotomy comes, in many many cases, from a feeling that it is not possible to live happily with both instincts. The bisexual is pulled both ways. He feels that he should make some firm decision about the direction of his sex life, and that decision, because of pressures and conditions quite outside himself, is invariably in favour of exclusive heterosexuality. But it is a hard decision to take, and even more difficult to abide by. In deciding to be one thing or another, the bisexual inevitably denies and suppresses one part of his nature, and this naturally causes conflict and tensions. All too frequently the decision is abandoned, and the bisexual drifts from person to person. He would be very happy, he says, to marry and settle down, but he can present a string of reasons why he is not ready to do so. Beneath them all lies the threat of his homosexuality. Consequently, the bisexual seldom feels able to trust himself, and prepares to let Nature take its course. The result is a growing dissatisfaction. The affairs become shorter, less fulfilling. The wish to love and be loved is surrounded by fear, and to protect himself the bisexual avoids any situation which might lead to a true emotional involvement. He remains immature, mistaking a prolonged and unnatural form of the adolescent "crush" or infatuation for love and compatibility.

Susan B's discovery of her bisexuality was particularly traumatic. She believes that she is a natural victim, and has consistently failed to reconcile the sexual impulse she feels towards both sexes. She is the only girl in a family with four boys. Because of her sex and the fact that she is the youngest, the early years were spent among devoted men. Her father worshipped her, her brothers were tender and loving. As a result, she thought that all men would treat her with a comparable consideration. She thought that her sex automatically ensured that she was "special", that men would woo and care for her, and that all sexual relationships with men would be an extension of her relationship with her brothers and father.

"When I was seventeen," she says, "I had my first sexual experience. I had met this boy at a local dance. He was good looking, nice, and I thought he was absolutely wonderful. None of my previous boy friends had done anything except kiss me and perhaps fondle my breasts, but this boy wanted a lot more. I was so overwhelmed by him that I must have been very easy to seduce. Anyway, we had sex together, and it was absolutely horrible. I knew nothing about men sexually, absolutely nothing. I had no idea the penis was so large and disgusting. Yes, it did disgust me. And he was very rough. He hurt me, and although I begged him to stop, he didn't listen."

Everything Susan B had learned about men was a contradiction of this boy's behaviour. The shock of the hard facts of sex was exaggerated for her. Where she had looked for an idealised romantic consummation, a gentle loving sense of protection, she found an animal-like need.

It was a very rude awakening, and one which led her to keep men at arm's length thereafter. In giving the boy her virginity, she believed that she was making a grand romantic gesture, but he simply used her body for his own ends.

For two years, Susan B's only sexual outlet was masturbation, and then she formed an intense relationship with an older woman.

"To make love with her was a perfectly natural outcome of the relationship. I realise that now. At the time I just let it happen. She was so kind to me, so warm and gentle, that I had no fear with her at all. Making love with her wasn't in a way connected with sex at all. To my mind, sex was exclusively concerned with being invaded by the horrid penis. But with her, everything was soft and tender. It felt beautiful."

But Susan B knew that lesbianism was frowned upon, if not definitely forbidden. She underwent a severe crisis of conscience and, faced with the prospect of being a confirmed lesbian, she broke off her relationship with the woman. She said:

"I couldn't bear the idea of being a lesbian, of being different from everyone else."

Eventually she met a man whose treatment of her seemed to tally with her ideal of male behaviour. Psychologically, she was ready for a heterosexual liaison, if only to prove that she was not a true lesbian. The man persuaded her to have intercourse with him and for a time things went beautifully. She felt that she had successfully overcome the fact of her lesbianism and had forsaken her fears of normal intercourse, although she still found the male organ ugly and unpleasant. But then the man broke off the affair, and a few months later married another woman.

"I was completely desolate," Susan B said. "In many ways this emotional rejection, just when everything seemed to be going so perfectly, was worse than my first experience. I felt that I could never trust a man again."

Again she turned to lesbianism, but the pattern repeated itself. After a time, the fear of the stigma of being "different" returned and Susan abandoned her friend, who attempted to commit suicide. This was almost as bad a shock as her own rejection by the man she had thought she loved. She realised now that lesbian relationships did not satisfy her emotionally, and since that time has been almost pathologically afraid of winning a woman's love, and equally frightened of committing herself to a man.

"I am cursed by an uncontrollable sexual desire," she says. "If it weren't for that, I'd never have sex at all. But sometimes I can't help myself, and yet any relationship I form is doomed to failure."

Susan B has never successfully reconciled herself to her bisexuality. Because of the circumstances of her discovery of her ability to enjoy lesbian relationships, she has never resigned herself to the fact that this tendency is a part of her nature. She traces the whole development back to her first heterosexual experience, and insists that her lesbian affairs have always been undertaken on the rebound and out of purely physical need. In a sense she disapproves of lesbianism, regards it as "wrong" and even "unnatural". Since she believes this, and yet is faced with her enjoyment of lesbian activities, a confusion results. Like so many bisexual women, she is unable to form a really satisfying emotional relationship with another woman. Her emotions are directed primarily towards men, whom she always expects to live up to the ideal of her brothers and father. With men who treat her approximately according to her expectations, she is clinging, over-emotional and dependent. Or rather she was. Now she cannot bring herself to get involved at all, and more tension results from this suppression of a natural emotional instinct.

Susan B's way of dealing, or rather seeming to deal,

with this problem is not uncommon among bisexuals. None of it is her fault, she has decided. She is simply cursed, doomed to unhappiness and failure. Both men and women betray her. She is certain of this. They either do not love her at all, or love her too much. Fundamentally she is a child, seeking the attention and undemanding concern of her family with adults who have needs of their own. By failing to accept that she is bisexual she has added to the problem. As far as she is concerned, she is a normal heterosexual girl who has been tricked into lesbianism by the cruel whim of fate. As is typical of the unreconciled bisexual, she regards her lesbian history as a threat to any relationship she might form with a man. In fact, she uses lesbianism as a defence, a last resort to ensure that she does not form a lasting heterosexual bond.

John P's awareness of his bisexuality occurred under unusual circumstances, and although his attitudes towards his sexual condition are unresolved, his remains a most instructive case.

"About three years ago, when I was sixteen, I had sex with my elder brother. It happened quite spontaneously, and although we had always been very close in a way I can't really explain, this was the very first time it had happened, although we had shared a bedroom all our lives.

"It happened because we were both feeling very sexy. He had been out with his girl friend, and had been petting heavily. I had been lying in bed looking at a girlie magazine. When my brother undressed, I saw that he had a big erection, and I suppose he saw me looking. I don't honestly know how it happened, but suddenly he was turning down the covers on my bed and getting in with me. We began to masturbate each other at once. And then he ran his hands all over my body and said I felt as soft and smooth as a girl.

"Quite honestly, it felt marvellous, and I just gave myself up to the situation. I don't know what prompted me because I had no homosexual experience at all, but suddenly I was using my mouth on him, and it really was the most marvellous experience of my life. When we were both satisfied, he just fell asleep in my bed, and in the morning, when I woke up, I found he was excited again, and immediately began to play with him. But he just pushed me away, and said that was enough."

Before this homosexual incident, John P had been sexually concerned entirely with girls, and although he had not actually had intercourse with a girl, he had indulged in various advanced forms of love play with them. After the event, he continued to go out with girls, but the sexual relationship with his brother did not cease. After a while, under similar circumstances, the events of that first night were repeated.

"After that, until he got married, it happened several times. Either when he had had a few pints, or when his girl had led him on, and then left him frustrated. On those occasions, he would let me do it to him."

Eventually the elder brother married. John P insists that he only married because the girl would not let him have intercourse with her under any other circumstances. John P has a violent dislike of his sister-in-law, and blames her for his brother's unhappiness. The marriage has not been particularly successful, largely, John P claims, because the wife is unwilling to permit intercourse at regular intervals. As a result, he has on two occasions "seduced" his brother since the marriage. He says proudly:

"What he can't get with her, he can always get with me."

Since the first homosexual incident, John P has had intercourse with a number of girls, but has formed no serious relationship with any of them. He tends to choose girls with loose morals whom he actively despises. He claims that all women are bitches, and only fit to be used for a man's relief. Significantly, he has had no homosexual contact with anyone other than his brother. He insists that he has not even considered the possibility and that if he were to receive homosexual advances from another he would reject them. Naturally, in the light of this it comes as no surprise that he regards himself as completely heterosexual. However, he can offer no explanation for his behaviour with his brother other than that brothers should help each other out, and similar quasi-sentimental statements.

John P's story is especially interesting because it shows quite clearly how the inevitably shocking discovery of homosexual potential can seriously affect and certainly shape the course of an individual's whole sex life. Further discussions revealed that John P had always been very proud of his brother, and had sought to emulate him. They have a great deal in common, their relationship is unusually harmonious and they confide a great deal in each other. From the onset of puberty John P had experienced erections when seeing his brother unclothed, but had not grasped the significance of this. Thus we have several indications that the brother occupied a very special and deeply valued place in the youth's life. When, on the spur of the moment, the brother allowed sex to enter their relationship, these feelings of fraternal admiration crystallised into a very real and powerful love. Quite simply, John P fell in love with his brother at the very moment when he was able to express that love sexually.

Significantly, John P has been the instigator of all the subsequent sexual events which have occurred between them. By his own admission, he learned to judge when the brother would be amenable to his approaches, and acted upon this knowledge. It is also noteworthy that subsequently the brother played a more and more passive role, and simply permitted John P to bring him to orgasm. Nor did the brother ever refer to these events or discuss them. Since his marriage John P's confidence has increased, and he is now able to invite his brother to indulge in homosexual practices, again using his knowledge to gauge when the brother is most frustrated as a result of his marriage.

John P's passionate love for his brother obviously explains his dislike of his sister-in-law. She is at one and the same time the girl who took his brother away from him, and the cause of his present unhappiness. He refuses to have anything to do with the wife, and cannot speak of her without insulting her. Once we understand this, his attitude to his own girl friends is immediately explained. He revenges himself on his sister-in-law via the girls he sleeps with. He is callous and brutal towards these girls, and deliberately chooses ones whom he can disparage.

John P's case is a particularly sad one. He rejects any suggestion of bisexuality, and refuses to accept that his relationship with his brother is truly homosexual. The fact that they are brothers, rather than adding to the abnormality of the relationships, makes it somehow acceptable in his eyes. But this relationship, ambivalent and surely doomed to end tragically, prevents him forming any reasonable relationship with another individual of either sex. John P is still very young, and there is hope that the situation may resolve itself, but at present there is no sign of this. He becomes daily more deeply involved with his brother, who turns to him more and more as his marriage becomes unhappier. Only by completely removing himself from the situation could John P hope to resolve it, but this he steadfastly refuses to do. He hangs on, hoping against hope for the day when his brother will leave his wife and return home, *i.e.* to him.

Unlike other bisexuals we have discussed, John P has succeeded in forming a satisfactory relationship, but it is largely one-sided and cannot be expected to thrive. Everything indicates that it must end in the rejection of John P by his brother. However, this is again a quite common pattern of bisexual behaviour. A lasting, strong love relationship is formed by the bisexual which immediately affects detrimentally the other aspect of his sexual nature. In John P's case, it is the heterosexual impulse which has been damaged. But even if the relationship formed is a hopeful one, *i.e.* is not doubly prohibited as John P's is, and is fully reciprocated, it is seldom free from danger. Bisexuals who form such attachments tend to be passionate and vigorous in their loving. They set an impossible code of fidelity for themselves which leaves part of their nature unsatisfied and repressed. They tend to become overdependent and demanding upon their lovers, who are not infrequently frightened off as a result. These passionate, apparently exclusive relationships seldom withstand the pressures the bisexual places upon them. Once they are ended, although deeply unhappy, often suicidal, the bisexual invariably feels relief. He or she is suddenly able to give their true natures a free rein without risk of damaging the relationship they so tenaciously prize. Inevitably they become promiscuous, moving from sex to sex in a frenetic search for the lover who has abandoned them. They seldom love again. Even if the possibility arises, such bisexuals are usually too afraid to commit themselves for fear of being hurt again, or for fear of their own needs. They remain restless and unhappy, living in emotional chaos and growing progressively more neurotic.

Louise M is a much more balanced example of the bisexual personality, but even she is not totally fulfilled. She says:

"I have always responded sexually to both men and women. Girls first, of course, because of greater opportunity. I really understand why men flip over girls. There is something so beautiful and harmonious about the female body that I don't know how anyone can fail to respond to it. I love to caress a girl's breasts, to stroke the smooth inside of her thighs. I'm said to be a really fantastic lesbian lover, and it certainly gives me a thrill too.

"As far as I'm concerned it's a perfectly natural response. Right from my teens I was attracted to girls, and my first experiences were with my own sex. I can't remember that I ever felt any guilt. I just reacted to all that beauty, and went about satisfying my urge. But I respond to men as well. I don't think men are as fundamentally attractive as women. Its more basic somehow, but the first time I saw a nude man with an erection, I reacted like any red-blooded woman. I love sex with men, but it is quite different with girls. Women are altogether more subtle. Sex with men is a basic animal act. There's nothing he can do with that great swollen thing but stick it up you. But with a girl there is time and opportunity for real subtlety and tenderness. Love making with a girl is an art, I think. With a man, it's a glorious animal function.

"Anyway, as far as my first experiences were concerned, I just drifted naturally into lesbianism without thinking about it at all. I was at boarding school, and then college, constantly in a predominantly female environment, and it never worried me at all. I had a whale of a time. But then other girls, even ones I was having sex with, started going out with boys and I didn't want to be left out. Girls are very competitive like that, you know. But I don't think I'd have deliberately sought out a boy if it hadn't been for the fact that all my friends were being dated and going moony over some boy. I was certainly getting plenty of sex, so it didn't worry me from that angle at all.

"But I got a date at last and found that a boy touching my breasts was just as good as a girl. Everything he did excited me, and bang, I was a virgin no longer. I've never been hung up about it at all. Man or woman, so long as they are good sex, it's all the same to me.

"At the moment I share a flat with a beautiful girl called Margaret. We both have good jobs and get on famously. Margaret is a natural blonde with a fantastic figure, and she's so sexy, you have no idea. We both have boy friends, but no one regular. Margaret and I have sex together two or three times a week, depending on the boy friend situation. But we always have it some time. And we have lots of boy friends.

"Frankly, I don't give a damn about love. It's never bothered me. Sex is what matters. Oh, I've shed a few tears over this one or that one, but I've never really been in love, and never felt that I want to be. I can't see me settling for one person all the time. What I like is to have a sort of regular relationship with one woman, and a variety of men on the side. The sort of arrangement I have with Margaret, in fact. But Margaret's too attractive to remain free for long. Definitely the marrying kind is our Maggie. I know it. I'm resigned to it. One day she'll up and go. No more sex with me. Settle down with a big strong husband and get pregnant. Quite honestly, there are times when I don't know what I'll do when that happens, but I know this much, it will happen, and I'll survive."

Despite her flippant exterior, Louise M is not a truly happy person. She gets a great deal out of life, is popular and amusing, but she is, as she well knows, doomed to a casual sex life. She is a remarkable example of a balanced bisexual. She takes everything in her stride, and suffers no qualms about her lack of moral attitudes. Truly it makes no difference whether it is men or women to her. But it is only possible for her to believe this because she cannot form any lasting attachment. In a sense, she is careless of other people, just as she is careless with herself. She is generous and warm hearted, but she can drop a lover overnight and behave badly to him or her if her attention is caught elsewhere. Like everyone else, she needs some measure of security, and this is usually supplied by women flatmates who act as a constant for her butterfly affairs with men. But what Louise M has already learned, and will probably always have to face, is that she is the ultimate loser. Flatmates and boy friends eventually go. In the final event, Louise M only has herself.

This, sadly, is often the fate of the apparently successful bisexual. They usually possess an amazing degree of self-knowledge and pretend to be glad that love does not concern them. They are disparaging about love and permanent relationships as a protection. Most of them know that there are lonely, desolate days ahead. As a result, they live in the present, their lives full of temporary distractions and amusements. It is, as Louise M says, a good way to live, but it can only last so long, and then the bisexual finds that he or she has to face a harsher existence which is all too often solitary.

Thus we see that although the bisexual's discovery of his peculiar sexual problem is not nearly so traumatic as that of other people with exceptional tastes, it is still a formative and important influence in many cases. As always, so much depends upon individual temperament and particular circumstances that it is dangerous to reach any too rigid conclusions about the growth of this awareness. But early experiences are always crucial, and much can be learned about the bisexual for this reason. We have now looked at some of the most common types of bisexuality, working forwards from their first discovery of their natures. The most striking fact to emerge from this examination is the frequency with which bisexuality leads to a life of virtual emotional barrenness. Often there are attendant sexual problems as well, but the task of reconciling and maintaining a workable balance between the opposite pulls of the two sexes is a formidable one, and we should not be too harsh in our judgement of the bisexual's failure to do this.

This essential problem is, of course, dramatically heightened by the society in which we live. Faced with an apparent choice, the bisexual cannot reach an unbiased decision. To deliberately elect to be primarily homosexual or lesbian is to place oneself, to a certain extent, outside society. Even in these more relaxed, liberal days there are many pressures on the individual to conform, and it is only logical that the bisexual should seek to opt for the most acceptable, and therefore easier, way of life. But the contrary urge persists, and no such decision can honestly be taken with any real degree of optimism. Ultimately the bisexual has to juggle and balance his sexual instincts, not only to satisfy himself, but to avoid hurting others. Today, with the growth of permissiveness and a general moral tolerance, the future looks more hopeful. Perhaps a time will come when the bisexual will not have to weigh the opinions of society in the balance, as well as his own needs. Perhaps soon he or she will be able to opt for what he or she truly is, a lover of both sexes, without coming under attack.

CHAPTER 3: THE ALL-ROUND LOVER

There are many barriers to sexual expression but when we say that, we are generally understood to mean barriers which are set up against the individual by some greater and usually remote authority. The law, of course, erects barriers, but these tend to have an indirect or localised effect. By far the most efficient curbs which are placed upon sexual expression are those which are formulated and accepted by the bulk of society. These, as we know, can be very powerful and their influence is great although they are seldom backed by official legislation. At the present, a great many of these social prohibitions are coming under attack. Some are crumbling, others are being modified to bring them up to date, and still more are subjects of fierce controversy. But even these mysteriously imposed yet influential barriers are not the last, or indeed the most difficult to overcome.

Even if he enjoys an almost unimagined degree of sexual freedom, the individual still has to face his own barriers in the form of inhibitions. Inhibitions are the last bulwark, the final safety valve, perhaps, which act as an autonomous check to complete freedom. In any discussion of prohibitions, inhibitions tend to be overlooked. It is fashionable to regard inhibitions as dangerous and lamentable attitudes. The word has come to imply that these are received attitudes, expressly designed to curtail freedom and limit potential. This view is certainly true of some inhibitions, but others are truly self-imposed, and herein lies their ultimate effectiveness. As such, they are a mark of man's responsibility, part of the complex mental process which distinguishes him from the instinctive animals, and because of this it is not wise to regard them as necessarily bad and wrong.

Inhibitions are self-imposed checks that are so deeply ingrained, so wholeheartedly accepted that the individual cannot easily ignore or overcome them. They can be divided into two main categories. In the first and most widely discussed, *i.e.* attacked, they are the embodiment of those social prohibitions we have already referred to. It is in this way that these exterior non-enforceable prohibitions gain their effectiveness. To put it at its most simple, society as a whole condemns a certain form of behaviour and because of the wish to conform, to be a respected, honourable member of society, the individual adopts this prohibition as his own and without question. Thus thereafter he acts as his own censor, and voluntarily limits his own potential in accordance with widely held views.

It is this fact of acceptance without question, without fully understanding the reason for the prohibition which makes some inhibitions dangerous and which has caused nearly all of them to fall into disrepute. The fact that they are, to all intents and purposes, independently held makes them so influential. But if we consider for a moment that society condemns any attempt by an adult to coerce a child into sexual acts, and accept that a great many individuals who feel a genuine attraction to children inhibit this instinct because of a fear of punishment and reprisals, we can see that inhibition is not necessarily a bad thing. Of course, it would be healthier and more pleasing if the individual reasoned on this point and refrained not because of fear but because he genuinely understood that such actions were dangerous to the child. But this is a matter for education and individual growth. In the meantime, it is better to curb through fear than not to prevent at all.

Other prohibitions, however, are less wise. Society

tends to reach unrealistic conclusions, particularly about personal sexual behaviour which, when adopted without question by the individual, can cut him or her off from a harmless but necessary means of sexual expression. When this situation arises, a person is truly inhibited and often deeply miserable. Today, fortunately, oral sex acts and sodomy between consenting partners are not regarded as dreadfully sinful. But in the recent past they were and fear of society's condemnation closed a whole area of acceptable sexual expression to a great many people, often resulting in frustration and tensions. These were truly bad inhibitions and are justly condemned.

But not all inhibitions are received in this way. Many are instinctive. A great many people limit themselves sexually and in other ways not because they have accepted that they should, but out of pure, inexplicable instinct. Such a person cannot explain why he or she feels this way, he can only insist that he does. Such inhibitions may be irrational, but they are not necessarily bad. Such inhibitions, although it is true that they limit and prevent, often act importantly as a symbol of security. It is popular, but erroneous, to believe that everybody actively requires a maximum amount of freedom. Many people simply are not equipped to deal with freedom on this scale. They need to narrow the possibilities of life down to an acceptable number and form. To them, confinements and barriers are not a prison but a protection. To sweep away these inhibitions can be traumatic in the extreme, and the results can be infinitely more serious than the effects of over-inhibition on others.

Thus we may say that, generally speaking, removal of an adopted inhibition is usually liberating, comparable to showing a child that there is nothing at all in the dark room. The removal of an instinctive irrational inhibition is a more hazardous process. It may reveal a whole new aspect of an individual's personality to him, and provided he is psychologically able to deal with this revelation, the effects are likely to be liberating. If he is not, there is a great danger of damaging tension, of self-loathing and disgust. Equally, such a revelation may come as a totally unpleasant shock. Self-knowledge is, in principle, a totally good thing, but only in principle. Some people can be overwhelmed by their potential, and the removal of such inhibitions can result in fear and disorientation which has far-reaching and unpleasant repercussions.

Inhibitions can be removed or overcome in a number of ways. Ideally the received inhibition is removed by prompting the individual to really think about his apparent belief, to examine it and genuinely consider its relevance to himself. If he can accept that the inhibited act need not make him feel guilty, the process is a truly liberating one, for fear of guilt, of having to live with guilt is the most powerful aspect of inhibitions. Ideally, instinctive inhibitions should not be removed but overcome by the individual. The role of an outsider in this situation is much more passive, primarily concerned with bolstering and confirming the individual's confidence. The individual must want to lose his inhibition, should be encouraged to do so, but it must be a personal experience. Such inhibitions are generally lost through example, through, in fact, conformity to a situation or mode of behaviour which is diametrically opposed to that which is ordinarily adhered to. This feeling of conformity, of doing what the other person is doing, is essential. There is safety in numbers. Any guilt will be equally shared. The instinctively inhibited are invariably timid and require the sense of being supported and protected by others.

Bisexuals have always been a prey to inhibition. Many have repressed their homosexual proclivities entirely out of a wish to conform. They are inevitably people who have been brought up to believe that any form of homosexuality is unnatural and sinful and frequently live among people who condemn homosexuality out of hand. The bisexual then has to try to conform, to stress his heterosexuality to the complete exclusion of the other instinct. He feels a sympathy towards the homosexual, but dare not defend him. Often he or she has great difficulty in forming the simplest relationship with a member of his or her own sex, and castigates himself or herself for any involuntary attraction he or she may feel.

Others are instinctively inhibited. They may live in a world where homosexuality is accepted and understood. Although they may know that there would be little dangers of their being ostracised or otherwise "punished" if their true nature was known, they cannot bring themselves to indulge in homosexual acts. Basically, such people do not trust themselves, are afraid of the unknown. They fear that once released, they will not be able to control the instinct, that even the slightest dabbling in homosexuality will cancel out their heterosexual impulse or will, in some mysterious way, change them. And, of course, they inhibit themselves instinctively, with all the usual resultant tensions and complexes. Occasionally, the process does work the other way around, *i.e.* heterosexual behaviour is feared and suppressed, but because of the universal acceptance of heterosexuality, this is very rare.

Because of these dual inhibitions, a great many bisexuals have never realised their full potential. Some have not even acknowledged the fact of their attraction to their own sex because the inhibiting process has been so strong and so quick. Others have persuaded themselves that their dual instinct does not really exist. They relegate their homosexual instincts to the realm of guilty fantasy and are generally deeply uneasy within themselves. Until comparatively recently, all but a handful of inhibited bisexuals stood little chance of being placed in a situation where, by example, they could find the courage to express their true nature without being filled with guilt and remorse. But now that position is rapidly changing and many people are making extraordinary discoveries about themselves with a minimum of detrimental effects.

In recent years, wife-swapping or sexual acts involving three or more people became a cult, a fashion. America is, by repute, the most active wife-swapping country in the world, but the activity is spreading throughout the West. Wife-swapping, to use its most popular and widely used name, although this is, very often, an inaccurate appellation, is the result of two main influences. It is, of course, a symptom of the movement for greater sexual freedom, for permissiveness. It is one way in which the individual or group can practise what they preach without much danger of reprisals. And what they preach is that people should please themselves about sex, should be free to indulge in any acts with willing partners in private, as long as these acts harm no one and are voluntarily entered into. Secondly, and equally importantly, wife-swapping may be seen as a direct result of the new understanding of sex. Sexologists and psychologists have admitted that sex, like everything else, grows stale, especially if it is confined to the same two people over a long period. Keeping the sexual side of a marriage alive has become a fashionable, serious "duty". But the dangers of jealousy and of adultery loomed large until some enterprising couples decided to mutually participate in their infidelities and thus avoid the danger. Again we see that there is safety in numbers.

Of course, many wife-swapping situations are strictly heterosexual and it should be clearly understood that wife-swapping does not automatically include homosexual behaviour. But equally it should be seen that when there are at least two people of the same sex involved in a sexual situation with a member or members of the opposite sex, the potential for homosexual behaviour exists. And since the essence of wife-swapping, of troilism and orgy situations is an abandoning of normal reticence, a freedom from inhibitions, it is not surprising that many such situations do naturally or deliberately lead to homosexual acts. Many swappers enter into the activity because they are latently bisexual. Since the object of the exercise, at least in theory, is to add spice to an exclusive sexual arrangement, if one member has a fantasy wish to partake in or to observe homosexual acts, this is a logical outcome of such situations.

Thus, to sum up, the orgy or swap situation is the logically ideal one for the bisexual. It is also frequently instrumental in revealing the latent bisexual, and in removing inhibitions which prevent the bisexual from realising or admitting his true potential. So let us now look at some of the bisexual swappers and see what happens when they are placed in a simulated free environment and situation, as well as studying the effects of this sudden liberation on them.

Janet R was, to all intents and purposes, a perfectly normal heterosexual girl. She had a rather aggressive exterior and deliberately gave the impression of being much less inhibited than she in fact was. When she went to work as Arnold K's secretary she faced a situation which is quite common among unattached young women. She found herself deeply attracted to her suave, handsome boss, and Arnold K made it quite clear that he found Janet equally attractive. Soon she accepted an invitation from her employer, and he took her out to dinner.

"Afterwards," said Janet, "in the car he began to make love to me. I had no wish to stop him. I found him terribly attractive and would have been a hypocrite to pretend that I had gone out with him quite innocently. But I had never been with a married man and I could not put this thought out of my mind. It wasn't, I'm afraid, that I felt guilty about his wife, not really, but I was concerned for myself. I didn't want to get involved in something that had no future, that was bound to end unhappily. I certainly had no intention of becoming the typical boss' mistress. So I made him take his hand out of my panties, although I was thoroughly enjoying what he was doing there, and asked him point blank, 'What about your wife?' Well, he was very casual and relaxed about the whole thing. He'd obviously been expecting me to ask some such question all evening. He said that Claire, his wife, knew where he was and who he was with. They had, he said, an 'arrangement', and there was no need for me to worry at all. When I pressed the matter, he said his wife knew him well enough to know that he would certainly try to have sex with me.

"Well, I just couldn't believe it. It all sounded much too much like a ready-made line to quieten my conscience. And I told him so. He nodded, and said that he'd expected me to say something of the sort, and therefore he'd take me home to meet his wife and I could see for myself.

"Of course I didn't want to go, but he started the car straightaway and ten minutes later, there we were. Claire was a real surprise. She is one of those dramatic redheads, beautifully groomed and dressed. Posh and expensive, you know, and with the sort of figure that would turn heads anywhere. I felt awful. Unsure of myself, scruffy, unsophisticated. But Claire was perfectly natural and did her best to put me at my ease. We had a couple of drinks, and then Claire stood up and said, 'Well, I'm for bed, and I expect you two are, as well. Have fun.' And off she went. Just like that."

In a few moments, the stunned Janet was upstairs with Arnold K who was skilfully undressing her. He countered all Janet's protestations by pointing out that she had seen for herself that Claire did not object to his sleeping with Janet. Soon his caresses overcame her reservations more skilfully than any words, and he and Janet lay naked on the bed together.

"But I couldn't do it," Janet said. "I just couldn't. I wanted to, I was aroused, but not enough. I just lay there like a block of ice, and when he asked me what the matter was, I had to say that I couldn't get used to the idea of having sex with him when I knew his wife was next door. He began kissing me and caressing my vagina, and slowly I began to thaw out a bit. And then suddenly I felt a movement on the bed and, a moment later, a tongue exploring between my thighs in the most exciting manner. I struggled upright, and looked down. Claire was lying between my legs, busily licking me. Before I had chance to say anything, Arnold began kissing me again, and I just gave myself up to the two of them."

Claire succeeded in rousing Janet where Arnold had failed, and the rest of the night was spent in alternate lesbian and heterosexual delights. Janet was completely won over, but the next morning was a difficult one for her. However, Claire took charge of the situation and explained to Janet that she and Arnold had reached a hiatus in their sex lives largely because of Claire's lesbian tendencies. Their solution to the problem was for Arnold to enjoy other girls, and to share them with his wife. Arnold himself was greatly excited by the sight of his wife performing cunnilingus on another woman and both partners insisted that there was nothing wrong in their behaviour.

"They were so persuasive," said Janet R, "so sophisticated and wordly. If I had objected, I would have sounded like a country bumpkin. And after all, nothing dreadful had happened. Everything was still the same and I had to admit that sexually I had enjoyed Claire as much as Arnold."

And so the three-way relationship has continued. Janet does not accept that she is bisexual. She justifies her part in these activities by her attraction to Arnold K and the fact that she always plays a passive role with Claire. Through a party given by the K's, Janet met and formed an apparently steady relationship with a young man who has also joined in these group sexual activities. But she continues to be pleasured by Claire, even though she insists that Arnold and the young man are the main reason for her continuing to participate in these gatherings.

Physically, Janet is deeply aware of Claire as a beautiful, enviable woman. She has already begun to consider taking a more active part in their lesbian sessions and everything suggests that her inhibitions are gradually being worn away. She was particularly worried by the young man's possible reactions if she performed cunnilingus on Claire. Like so many unresolved bisexuals, Janet finds the passive role excusable and since she has no wish to be thought a lesbian, is afraid of the young man's reactions. However, everything suggests that he is fully aware of the true situation and can probably reassure Janet on this point. In time, she will probably be completely uninhibited, and in that case it is better that her prospective boy friend should be fully aware of her nature so that she does not feel that her lesbian tendencies threaten her relationship with him.

In some ways, Janet R is fortunate that Arnold and Claire were able to help her over the crisis of reaction she experienced as a result of that first night with them. But she is, perhaps, less fortunate in that there appears to have been no need for the removal of her inhibitions. Discovering her lesbian potential does not really help Janet because she was already quite happy. However, if she can form a proper relationship with this young man, it seems likely that she will suffer no serious effects from this discovery, but will have extended the range of her sexual pleasure. Her case is one of awakening tendencies which were causing no problem. Fortunately, Janet seems to be equipped to cope with this new knowledge of herself and with care will probably not suffer any serious effects from what must yet be regarded as an unnecessary situation.

At forty, Clive D was a genuine repressed bisexual. Although happily married to an attractive woman five years his junior, he was nervous, moody and depressed. For a long time, the sexual side of the marriage had been unsatisfactory. His wife, Helen, said:

"Clive just didn't seem to be interested in sex. It was the classic situation one reads about, except that this time it was the husband who was always too tired or didn't feel like it. I didn't object to having to rouse him, but even when I succeeded, he left me unsatisfied. It was a hopeless situation."

Helen D is a highly sexed woman, as well as being a very intelligent one. As her marriage grew increasingly difficult because of mutual sexual frustration, she did not dissolve into tears, but tried to approach the problem in a constructive, adult way. Helen D had read about wife-swapping, and she decided that the only thing wrong with their marriage was that sex had become a habit for Clive. It needed, she thought, perking up. But Helen D did not suggest swapping to her husband, she merely announced, in a very forthright manner, that she intended to take a lover.

"I was completely stunned," said Clive, "but also instantly excited. Without hesitation, the first thing I said was, 'Very well, but you'll have to let me join in.' To my amazement, Helen agreed, and the subject was dropped. I never thought Helen would mention it again. You see, we both *could* have been joking."

Clive D's reaction was based on a fantasy wish. As a young man, he had had a number of homosexual contacts, but these had ceased the moment he met Helen. Over the years he had been shocked and disturbed to find that he was continually drawn to young men, deeply attracted to them.

"I used to look at young men and imagine all sorts of things. I remember once sitting in my parked car for over an hour watching a group of young labourers on a building site. It was summer and they were all stripped to the waist. I was terribly excited, but I never did anything. I couldn't. I felt disgusted with myself. I'm not one of those men who thinks that homosexuality is wrong, but I believed it was wrong for me. I thought such a thing would kill Helen. It could easily ruin my career and affect our social life. And it seemed such a betrayal of Helen. I had always been a faithful husband and to turn queer on her seemed to me worse than a hundred normal infidelities."

But the desire persisted, and his sexual relationship with Helen grew worse. Thus, when Helen delivered her ultimatum, although Clive did not dare to take it seriously, he saw an opportunity to indulge at least a part of his desire. A part only, because he insists that when he imagined Helen with a lover, he only saw himself as an observer, not a participant. The idea, however, excited him greatly.

Helen continued:

"I was absolutely serious. I was at the end of my tether and was so frustrated I was prepared to do anything. But I loved Clive and wanted to stay with him. I couldn't, and still can't, contemplate real wife-swapping. I couldn't bear to see or know that Clive had been with another woman. I suppose that means I'm possessive. Certainly I'm very jealous.

"Anyway, I needed sex, and my motive was to inspire Clive to give it to me. I thought that if Clive saw me with another man, a young virile man, he'd be so enraged he'd be a proper husband to me again. That's why I agreed to his participating. After that it was quite simple. By that time I felt I had nothing to lose, and I suppose I thought that after fifteen years of marriage we ought to be able to cope with any tensions that arose. So I put an ad in one of those personal contact magazines. I said Clive and I wanted a single young man, and so we met Jack."

Helen received many replies, and selected three possible candidates. She finally settled for Jack after an exchange of letters which satisfied her that he was the right sort of young man. Meanwhile, although the matter had not been referred to, Clive continued to think about the prospect of Helen taking a lover with his knowledge, and the fantasies he wove around the situation greatly excited him. There was, as a result, a slight improvement in their sex life.

And then Clive D returned home one evening to find Jack having a pre-dinner drink with Helen. She introduced Jack calmly as her intended lover. Jack, a physical training instructor, attracted Clive at once, and Helen, with the consummate ease of a born and practised hostess, soon had the two men chatting comfortably together. She kept their glasses filled, and after dinner led Jack to the bedroom. Clive sat alone for a few minutes, trying to resist the temptation to follow them. He reasoned that Helen had every right to have a lover, for he had failed her as a husband. He felt that he had no right to intrude. But the situation was too tempting. All evening he had been excited by the unusual situation and had been wondering what Jack looked like undressed.

Clive D stood in the open bedroom door and watched with mounting excitement. Helen lay naked on the bed, her ample charms well displayed. Jack stood in his underpants beside her, the evidence of his excitement quite obvious. With bated breath, Clive watched the young man remove his last garment and begin to kiss and caress Helen. He moved into the room and avidly watching, began to undress. Slowly, Jack planted kisses along the length of Helen's gleaming body, and then began to excite her with his tongue. Tentatively, a mesmerised Clive reached for the young man's swollen organ. Momentarily, Jack raised his head and smiled encouragement at the trembling but deeply excited man.

"And we've never looked back," said Helen. "Mind you, there was a nasty moment there when I thought I was going to be left out in the cold, but eventually, both of them made love to me. By then I'd got the message. It all fell neatly into place. And as soon as Jack had gone, I faced Clive with it. I knew he would be feeling awful, but we had to clear it up." Clive added to this:

"Helen was marvellous. I told her everything. The incidents before I met her, the longings I had never dared admit. She understood perfectly, and we ended up by making love. There have been several other men since. We still place ads, and once we had two bisexual young men at the same time. But even if we go months without having a swap session, we are all right sexually now. I only have to think of the wonderful times we've had to be able to satisfy Helen completely."

There can be no doubt about the beneficial effects of this behaviour on Clive D and on his marriage. His inhibitions about homosexuality have been successfully removed. With his wife blatantly taking pleasure with another man, a sense of freedom is gained. Suddenly, anything seems acceptable. His fears about homosexuality are successfully allayed because he is also partaking in a heterosexual situation, can make love to his wife to prove his masculinity. Helen's attitude is also very helpful for she accepts this aspect of her husband's sexual impulse frankly and calmly. She still loves and wants him, and her behaviour proves this.

Bisexual men who enjoy a satisfying heterosexual relationship are generally inhibited about their homosexual propensities. These are most successfully removed if the wife or mistress can be involved in the activities which take place. In this way the man avoids the suggestion, at least to his own satisfaction, of true homosexuality. The acts are reduced to a simple variation, and he needs the presence of the woman in order to be able to prove his heterosexuality as well. However, ideal as the situation is, it is not always so simply reached. Unfortunately, all wives are not as relaxed and understanding as Helen D. Doreen Y, for example, sought advice after a swapping incident which had greatly upset her. She obtained an interview with a psychiatrist who made these details available, not only on her own behalf, but also for her friend, Joan W.

"You see, doctor," she said. "Joan and me have been wife-swapping. Oh, that sounds silly, doesn't it? What I mean is, me and my husband, Tony, have swapped around with my friend Joan and her Bill. You see, we'd all read about swapping and that in the papers and one night we got to talking about it over a few drinks and Tony, he says, 'Well, I wouldn't mind having a bit with Joan, anytime.' He's terrible like that, is Tony, after a few pints. Well, we all laughed, you know, but blow me if Bill didn't say, 'That's all right mate. While you're doing that, I'll look after Doreen.' That's me.

"Well, anyway, that's how it started. The two blokes just started kissing us and feeling us up and that and before we knew where we were I was in bed with Bill and Tony had Joan on the settee. But that's not the problem, you see, because it was lovely. Everything was o.k. No jealousy or nothing. And afterwards we all got together in the sitting room stark naked, and it wasn't at all embarrassing or anything. We all felt very, well, you know, free.

"Anyway, after a bit Bill and Tony said they were hungry, so me and Joan go off to the kitchen to make some sandwiches. Of course, we talked about the fellows, but then me and Joan have never had no secrets from each other, and it was all a bit of a laugh really. So, anyway, when we've got the sandwiches done, we goes back into the sitting room, and honestly I could have died of shame. You see, Tony was on his knees, kneeling like, in front of Bill, and he was well, he was sucking his thing.

"Well, that finished it. I just burst into tears, and Joan,

she was furious. She got dressed and had Bill out of there before you could snap your fingers. And of course it was worse for me because it was my chap who'd been doing it. Joan and me are still friends, but she won't come near Tony. She says he must be queer and he's out to turn her Bill that way. I just felt awful and wouldn't let Tony touch me for days. But he says as how Bill did it to him, and I told Joan this and she says Bill said so too. Well, they wouldn't both tell a lie like that, would they? Only now we don't know what to think and everything's horrible. Joan says perhaps they're both queer, and all we can do is keep them away from each other. But it's horrible thinking you've got a husband like that, and I don't feel the same with Tony. I mean, how could they do something like that?"

Doreen Y's case might be regarded as an example of what happens when people involve themselves in a situation for which they are not equipped. From what she said, it seems obvious that both she and her friend regarded the whole swap situation as a rather risqué but acceptable joke. The men were the prime movers in creating the situation and they undoubtedly responded more wholeheartedly to the uninhibited freedom of the situation. Bill and Tony both told their distressed and angry wives that they had, when left alone together, been talking about their wives as sexual creatures and lamenting the fact that neither of them would consent to perform fellatio. This had excited them both, and when Bill offered to do it to Tony if he would return the favour, neither of them saw anything wrong in the act. When the women returned and interrupted Tony's performance, the situation immediately became dramatised out of all proportion.

From all that the doctor could learn, there seems to be no reason to regard Bill and Tony as anything other than normal healthy heterosexuals. Neither has had anything but the usual adolescent experiences of homosexuality and there is nothing besides this isolated incident to suggest that they are bisexual. They are, however, very curious about sex. They thoroughly enjoyed the swap experiment and responded to the uninhibited atmosphere by experimenting further with mutual fellatio. Had their wives' reactions been different, more homosexual acts might have developed, but as it is, instead of the swap situation acting as a liberating agent, it has broken their friendship and adversely affected their sexual relations with their wives. Joan and Doreen are utterly unreconcilable to any form of male homosexuality, and although the doctor was able to reassure them of their respective husbands' normalcy, a veto has been placed on any repetition of the events of that evening. Things are, more or less, back to normal, but a nagging doubt exists in both women's minds, and having had a taste of the freedom and pleasures of swapping, the husbands may not long be content to accept their wives' ruling.

Very strange things can happen in situations in which a number of people come together for sexual purposes. This was proved by the very unusual case of Jane G. At the age of sixteen, Jane G became pregnant as the result of a casual affair with a boy of the same age. Consequently, Jane underwent an abortion which proved to be a very traumatic experience which even now, some five years later, she cannot recall without distress. Afterwards, Jane determined to have nothing more to do with men. Eventually, she drifted into a lesbian situation which she enjoyed. This seemed to be the answer to her problem. Jane liked sex, and only her exaggerated fear of pregnancy prevented her seeking it with men. But this fear was pathological, although she soon found that despite her vow, she was strongly attracted to men. However, she also enjoyed the "glamour" of being a lesbian. She made no secret of her tastes, and mixed with a semi-bohemian crowd who accepted such things calmly. Jane had several lesbian lovers and eventually formed a reasonably permanent relationship with a girl of her own age. It was with this girl that Jane went to a party given by one of the discotheque crowd she went around with.

The party developed into an orgy, without this having apparently been planned. One couple started to pet heavily. Another followed suit and soon both clothes and inhibitions were shed. Jane and her girl friend had both had plenty to drink, and soon Jane began to make love to her friend. This spectacle attracted several observers, and one young man began to join in. At first, Jane tried to prevent him, but the crowd shouted her down. Jane depended very much on the good opinion of her friends, and soon she was watching her lesbian partner in the throes of sexual ecstasy with a man. The sight excited Jane very much, and when another young man made advances to her, she offered only token resistance. Soon Jane had forgotten her fears and was revelling in the skilled love-making of her partner.

Afterwards, of course, Jane was almost hysterical with fear in case she had been made pregnant. But at last her period arrived and she was faced with the fact that she had thoroughly enjoyed the experience. With typical bravado, Jane obtained a supply of contraceptive pills, and began to look at men with an entirely new eye.

"I honestly don't believe," said Jane, "that it would ever have happened if it hadn't been for that orgy. Men had tried to make me, and I always froze up and fought them off. You see, in my mind all that ghastly business of the pregnancy and the abortion had become muddled up with the sex act itself. I'd completely forgotten how super sex is. All I'd remembered was the pain. But that night, that boy gave me a whole string of orgasms that no girl has ever managed to rival. Now, with the aid of the Pill, I feel completely uninhibited."

It is very unusual for an individual to accept the deviated side of their nature in this way, but Jane G's reasons are convincing. She is a genuine bisexual, and now enjoys both sexes quite happily. In the circle in which she moves, such practices are openly approved and even encouraged. Happily, Jane seems to have adjusted well to her dual sexual nature.

How do the bisexuals themselves react to the swap phenomenon? At this particular time, the adventurous bisexual has an unprecedented opportunity to indulge his tastes, but does he seize it and welcome it?

"I've always known that I was bisexual," said Kenneth W, "and for my money the personal contact ads and swapping are the answers to a bisexual's prayer. At first I used to answer ads. They used to be in a minority, but you could always find one or two couples or groups who wanted a single man. But now I advertise myself and just pick the best. If I were to take up all the offers I receive from one ad, I'd be a physical wreck in a few weeks. The best thing about swapping and group sex is that it creates a situation where the bisexual is accepted. It gets rid of that hole in the corner feeling that can blight a lot of your sex life if you really want to perform in both directions."

Logically, of course, the group situation is the *ideal* one for bisexuals. If a man or a woman really enjoys sexual acts with both sexes, then the opportunity to indulge in both at the same time should represent a sort of paradise. The effect on the bisexual is roughly equivalent to that of a heterosexual man being suddenly placed in a room full of nubile, willing women. But this can only really be true for the well balanced, totally accepting bisexuals, such as Ron V, an enthusiast who dotes on group sex.

'Everywhere you look there is something to turn you on. If you respond to both sexes then what could be more exciting than to be in a room full of girls and boys stark naked and really going at each other?"

But for other bisexuals, it is the presence of the opposite

sex which makes group situations so desirable. This does not mean that they are not attracted to their own sex, but that the presence of the opposite sex helps to remove their inhibitions, to make their homosexuality acceptable.

Sheila A says:

"I'm bisexual, but I'm sort of nervous about going with women. I never touch a woman unless a man is present. I suppose its silly but something about a man watching me really excites me. This way, lesbian acts are reduced to the level of foreplay. It excites the girls and the man, but the outcome is always heterosexual intercourse, and that's the way I like it."

Partly, this feeling is based on a natural fear of being caught out in homosexual acts, in being regarded as a confirmed homosexual. The willingness to indulge in heterosexual activity symbolically destigmatises the homosexual practices.

But other bisexuals are not at all in favour of group activity. To enjoy both sexes at once is not at all their idea of bliss. Many insist that sex is private, should be shared solely between two people. But their objections often go further than this obvious one. They value the difference in quality and emotion which they experience with the different sexes. They want to enjoy men entirely, and women. The mixing of the two, consequently, does not appeal. Generally, bisexuals who feel like this have little difficulty in reconciling themselves to the implications of their homosexuality. To them it is the orgy situation which is unpleasant and forbidden. In many ways this attitude may be understood as an attempt to conform within the unconventional urges of their nature. It is, very largely, a matter of one's own attitudes and beliefs. To some, the private homosexual act is untenable. Only in group situations are the fears and hesitations overcome. For others, the converse is true.

Many people are anxious to leap to the defence of the

swappers. Most of these defenders are almost evangelical in their insistence upon the therapeutic values of group and shared sexuality. Indeed, one might be forgiven for thinking that the swappers' only motives are therapeutic ones, although this is, of course, nonsense. But the practice is in keeping with current advanced moral standards. The swappers do behave responsibly within the situation and at a time when personal freedom is paramount, it is difficult to condemn them. Certainly they have been instrumental in helping the bisexual to come to terms with himself and, in many cases, to lead a fuller life. Often it only requires the borrowed confidence of a group of uninhibited people to reveal the bisexual to himself, and more often than not he feels relieved and gratefully free from a nagging tension he has not fully understood. But not always.

Michael C attended an impromptu swap session, but with unpleasant after effects.

"It was fine," he said, "at first. We were all friends together anyway, and we were all slightly drunk. It just sort of happened, and soon everyone was having sex with anyone they liked. It was exhilarating. I suddenly found myself thinking how right all this hippy philosophy was. I suddenly realised that one did want, desire, call it what you like, lots of people and that if that is the case then one should be quite natural, and just do it. There was nothing sordid about those couples making love. It was natural, beautiful and exciting. I had the fiancée of a close friend of mine, a girl I'd always liked and admired. I mean, I'd fancied her, and it was just great. It really was.

"Afterwards, I got up to get a drink. Most of the couples had finished, but there were still one or two at it. I was just standing there, watching, feeling great. Suddenly, this one fellow, I didn't know him very well, started to join in with one of the couples who were still making love. Even that seemed o.k. He was caressing them, and sucking the girl's breasts and so on. You could see it added to their pleasure, and there was no doubt about how it excited him. Well, it excited me too, and suddenly the friend whom I have already mentioned, the one whose girl I'd had, began to... to touch me. I froze, literally. And then I started to tremble. I pushed his hand away. I thought he must be joking. But he began again. I told him to stop it, but he just said that this was a free for all and since I'd enjoyed his girl I'd have to let him enjoy me. Suddenly he was using his mouth on me, and I was responding in spite of myself. I just shut my eyes and stood there. The moment I had ejaculated, I rushed out of the room, washed myself thoroughly, dressed and left.

"I felt absolutely disgusted. I still feel dirty, even now. I don't understand how he could have done it, or how I came to let him. I can't face any of the people who were there that night. I mean, they saw. They all must think I'm queer. I hate myself for letting him do it. There's no excuse for me, really. I should have punched him one. I can't think why I didn't, except perhaps that he was a friend of mine, someone I was fond of. And, of course, I had had his girl."

Investigations revealed that Michael C had marked, if unrealised, bisexual tendencies. These had been demonstrated to him in what is normally regarded as the most acceptable way, but he rejects them. Later, he admitted that the experience was one of the best he had ever had, from a physical point of view, and this intense enjoyment obviously runs counter to his beliefs about himself. He is terrified of being thought a homosexual in any way. But he has learned that sexual pleasure is not dependent upon what one wishes. Now he struggles with himself, has severed himself completely from his friends and is extremely unhappy. It can only be hoped that the trauma of the discovery of his bisexuality will be resolved, for at the moment it is impossible to regard the discovery as anything but unfortunate. Michael C has undertaken a course of analysis which, hopefully, may serve to resolve his fears, and may perhaps reveal more convincing reasons for his exaggerated rejection of his homosexual propensities.

So we see that the bisexual's experience of and reaction to group sex varies considerably. However, in the majority of cases, the effects are beneficial. As a result, the bisexual is sought by swappers and group sex enthusiasts, even when they themselves are not bisexually inclined. The bisexual is valuable because he is a natural performer, one who can be counted on to produce some novel twist to the group proceedings. But this role is unlikely to last for, in the uninhibited atmosphere of these situations, more and more people are finding themselves drawn to bisexual behaviour. The true bisexual is beginning to play the role of the catalyst, to bring out undiscovered desires in others. Whether these people are truly bisexual or not remains to be seen. At present it seems likely that their sporadic flirtation with their own sex under special circumstances are more accurately a manifestation of variety-seeking rather than evidence of true bisexuality. But one thing is certain, the groups and the swappers are inevitably creating a situation in which bisexuality will become the norm. Not only does the true bisexual flourish under such conditions, not only is the latent bisexual revealed, but the so-called exclusive heterosexual stands a strong chance of discovering that sexual pleasure can be taken with his or her own sex without unpleasant consequences necessarily resulting.

CHAPTER 4: THE BISEXUAL WOMAN

Mary F has only the dimmest recollection of her mother for she died while Mary was still a toddler, but she knew instinctively that the step-mother her father proudly presented to her could never take the place of a true mother. Like so many children who are, for one reason or another, deprived of one parent, Mary erected a fantasy of motherhood which it would have been impossible for any woman to embody. Wisely, her step-mother did not try, but contented herself with making a home and caring for Mary in a practical way. This attitude obviously contributed to the establishment of an equable relationship between the two. Mary did not dislike her step-mother, nor was she able to love her. By not seeking to occupy a special maternal place in Mary's emotional life, the step-mother avoided the resentment which so many children feel in similar circumstances.

But against this outwardly calm background, the dream of an ideal, a deeply loving and passionately wanted mother, persisted. As Mary grew older, however, her idea of a mother changed, became more of an elder sister, someone to whom Mary could turn for help and guidance, someone who would love her but be able to share in her preoccupations. At the age of eighteen, Mary won a scholarship which took her to one of the older established universities, and there, in Katharine P, Mary met her ideal.

In her late thirties, Katharine P was a brilliant and respected scholar, a quietly beautiful, obsessively neat woman. She was, in Mary's eyes, totally admirable. She was obviously beautiful, where Mary was not. She knew infinitely more about the things which attracted Mary than the girl ever dared to hope to learn. She had a cool, even chilling and remote manner which Mary's appealing, vulnerable gaucherie quickly penetrated to reveal a warm personality, brusquely kind but very tender.

"I worshipped her," reflected Mary, "because she was so much like the sort of woman I'd always imagined my mother would have been. She was sophisticated, cultured and gentle. She was so assured. Beside her, I was a mess. Her white skin and thick jet-black hair made her look like one of the statuesque heroines of a Romantic novel. And she was something of a mystery. I remember thinking that she must have been cruelly disappointed in love. One really thought in those sort of clichés at that age, and this made her all the more attractive."

Katharine P was appointed Mary's tutor in her first year, and very soon Mary discovered that she could talk to her as she had never talked to anyone. She poured out her soul to a patient, sympathetic Katharine who made her feel that her hopes and her fears were worthy of mature consideration. Consequently, Mary was elated when Katharine invited her to spend part of the long vacation in France with her. A cultural tour had been planned which would help Mary with her studies, but most importantly, it would enable Mary to be with the woman she had already begun to love.

"We went to a small town in Normandy on our first night. Katharine so chic and quietly elegant, and me in an unsuitable summer dress with loads of rustling petticoats underneath. We shared a room. I remember being a little surprised at this, but I was relieved as well. I hated being separated from her for even a few hours. And while I struggled with my flounced petticoats and my preposterous uplift bra, Katharine coolly undressed. I know I stared at her body. I couldn't help it. Her skin was like alabaster, and when she unpinned her hair it fell in great black waves over her shoulders. Her breasts were firm and high with small pink nipples, like those of a young girl. She had wide, flaring hips and long smooth legs. She was like a statue, beautiful and remote.

"Suddenly she came over to me, completely naked, and I felt her calm capable fingers helping me with the stubborn catch of my bra. She slipped it off and turned me round to face her. My breasts brushed against hers and I saw that her nipples became erect. 'You know, Mary,' she said in her perfectly modulated, rather deep voice, 'You are a very attractive girl.' I don't know what happened, but something burst inside me. This touch of kindness, this simple compliment made me suddenly feel human at last. I burst into floods of tears, burying my face in her naked breasts. It was a sign, somehow, that she cared for me, and as I wept on her bosom, it was like having a mother at last. The way she stroked my hair and comforted me, somehow that was what I'd always wanted. Then she raised my red and blotchy face and kissed me, very gently.

"She persuaded me to get into bed, and then she asked if I would like her to stay with me. There was nothing I wanted more, and suddenly she was lying beside me, and I could feel her cool white body against mine. She stroked my hair, kissed me again, and then she began to run her hands very lightly over my breasts. Soon she had slipped off my panties and I felt her fingers brushing my sex. I didn't stop to think what was happening, I just let it happen. I loved her. I would have done anything for her and she made me feel marvellous. Later, she threw back the bedclothes and lay on top of me, moving her body against mine. I had a shattering climax, and shortly afterwards she went quite rigid and cried out. Afterwards, she lay between my thighs and performed cunnilingus on me. It was the first time I'd realised such practices existed, and it gave me immense pleasure. We were lovers from that night on. Katharine was a very passionate woman beneath her cool exterior and she introduced me to everything two women can do together. One afternoon, in Paris, she went off by herself, and she returned with a dildoe. She used it on me, and taught me to use it on her. That was good, too, but best of all I liked the sensation of her tongue on my vagina."

That vacation was a virtual crash course in lesbian sexual practices for Mary. She was receptive to them all, for Katharine could do no wrong in her eyes and her mature body was ripe for sexual experiences which, until then, she had never had. As a result, Katharine became everything Mary wanted, a cultured, wise teacher, a warm loving mother-figure, and a passionate lover. Mary felt that her life was complete and fulfilled.

When she returned to university in the autumn, Katharine P was no longer Mary's tutor. They met secretly in Katharine's flat, but she insisted that Mary be cautious and circumspect about their relationship. At the end of the academic year, another holiday took place, but during this trip Katharine announced that she had been given a sabbatical year and that she would be going to America in the autumn. Mary was deeply upset and this reaction was ultimately damaging to their relationship. It showed clearly the depths of Mary's dependence on her mentor. Katharine was a mature woman who cared about her career. She was also basically unfitted for the role of mother substitute in which Mary had inevitably cast her. She became impatient with Mary's hysterical tears and reminded her that there was more to the world than hiding in another's skirts. To Mary, those necessary words sounded brutal and only added to her despair, but out of her love for Katharine, she promised to work hard and sit her finals.

"I lived for her letters throughout that last year. Without them I think I would have been sunk. But they weren't the sort of letters I wanted. Katharine was too careful for that. But I managed somehow, and got quite a good degree. I'd hoped, of course, to see Katharine as soon as our terms ended, but she wrote to say that she was spending the summer in Canada. Again I was desolate. I'd decided to do an M.A. at another university and so there was no immediate pressure on me. I went to France, staying in all the places I'd been on that first trip with Katharine. A sentimental journey I suppose you'd call it, but it wasn't a success. I didn't feel particularly sad, and certainly not elated. After a week, I was quite simply bored, so I took off for the Riviera.

"I still hadn't been with a man. But on the Riviera you can't avoid them. Everywhere I looked there were half-naked suntanned men, and I found them terribly disturbing. It was like a second puberty. I suddenly realised that men were different from girls, and I was intrigued by the difference. And I felt terribly lonely. I knew no one. I was conspicuously the only girl on the *plage* who didn't have an attentive admirer. So I stopped being coolly frigid and British, and when André blatantly tried to pick me up, I let him. I don't know why. Partly I wanted someone to talk to, and partly because he was twenty, dark, handsome and made me feel like a woman.

"I was putty in his hands, of course. We had lunch together, and then I went back to his room. He was like a little boy, gay and charming, chattering away. He wanted to show me his books, his records. Well, I went, and when he started to kiss me, I let him. I allowed him to caress me, undress me, and for the first time in my life I stared at a male erection. He made love to me, but it wasn't a success, not from my point of view. I was used to Katharine's gentle, feminine approach. I realised that afternoon why women say that men are beasts. He bit my nipples cruelly hard, and he forced his penis so roughly up into me, that I thought I'd faint. It was another kind of love-making altogether. I wasn't disgusted or put off or anything, but I was sort of clinically detached. I was so inexperienced, that part of the trouble was that I couldn't relax. I really didn't care about it one way or another, but André seemed satisfied, and I let him do it again."

Soon Mary drifted into the company of another of the beach-roving young men. This one used a more subtle approach. Before having intercourse with her, he performed cunnilingus and Mary experienced an orgasm which prepared her body for proper coitus. With predictable emotionalism, Mary fancied that she loved this youth, and stayed with him for the rest of her holiday. But eventually they had to part, and the man made it quite clear that their relationship was nothing more than a summer romance. Mary retreated to her new university to lick her wounds.

"Now my problem," she continued, "was recognisably sexual. The ideal of a woman like Katharine was still my goal, but I think I'd begun to realise that this was a pipe dream. I had a sort of affair with another girl there, a research student who was definitely lesbian. But I couldn't feel about her as I had about Katharine. She was too young and we were pretty well-matched intellectually. There was nothing remotely maternal about her. It was a very casual relationship. We didn't talk about it much. Just sometimes we had sex together. But I started going out with one of the third-year male students, and she hated that. She had a sort of phobia about men. But I still found them very attractive, and in my own quiet way I suppose I was fairly promiscuous. But it never seemed to work out. Always, one came to depend more and more on sex, and then one of us would lose interest. I'd perhaps go back to the girl for a bit, but it was a pretty indefinite and inconclusive pattern. I was quite glad when I left really."

Mary F now has a good job in a government department. She is thirty years old, unmarried and sees little prospect of settling down in any permanent relationship. The pattern established in her last year at university has continued over a period of years. Mary has had a number of love affairs, with both men and women. But, as she succinctly puts it, "it never seemed to work out." Mary tends to have more relationships with men than women, but this is largely because her affairs with men are generally of very short duration. More importantly, none of these relationships, lesbian or otherwise, fulfil her other than on a simple sexual level. And Mary, because she is easily satisfied sexually, soon grows bored with this aspect of a relationship, and seeks variety.

In so far as it is at all possible to talk of a "typical" bisexual woman, Mary F meets most of the requirements. Her dual sexual nature is not a symptom of the sensation-seeking promiscuous woman, but of a deep emotional unrest which has been greatly influenced by circumstances beyond her direct control. This is very often a facet of female bisexuality, whereas a great many male bisexuals, largely because of their animalistic approach to sex, fall into the category of pleasure seekers. The impulse which initially motivated Mary's behaviour and which still underpins her emotional loneliness, is her motherlessness. Mary's childhood was, in comparison to that of many other women, extremely secure and uncomplicated. But it was clouded and influenced by her lack of a true mother. Her search for sexual and emotional fulfilment has consequently been a search for an idealised, unattainable mother-figure. This again is a fairly common phenomenon. Simply because she has always been intensely aware of not having the love of a true mother, her whole attitude to emotional relationships has become inextricably interwoven with this lack. And since in a mature woman the emotional aspect of love is inseparable from sexual expression, she has always been drawn on by the chimera of a mother/lover combined. In Katharine P she came as close as she is likely to do in reaching her ideal, but, as she herself has come to see, Katharine P was not a natural mother surrogate, but a full-blooded lover. Mary F understands now that her insistence on casting Katharine in the mother role was instrumental in the break up of the affair.

Mary's behaviour with Katharine shows genuine immaturity, as does her reference to a "second puberty" when she first became aware of men as attractive physical creatures. This is a very perceptive phrase, one which indicates Mary F's unusual grasp of her own problem. Her immaturity, though lamentable, is an almost inevitable outcome of her personality and childhood situation. Nor need it be crippling, as is shown by the development Mary has herself made. She sees now that any relationship which met her ideal requirements would be a false one. Few women would be both a lesbian lover and a doting mother. And Mary realises, too, that at thirty she must learn to stand on her own feet. She is certainly too old to be dependent on a mother she stands little chance of finding.

Not surprisingly, all Mary's "serious" lesbian relationships have been destroyed by her need for a mother. Women who have been genuinely fond of her, sexually involved with her, have found her clinging, childishly emotional dependence insupportable. Other casual relationships have either been destroyed because of her persistent association with men, which few lesbians find completely acceptable, or by lack of any true effort to maintain the relationship. Indeed Mary's realisation that she is not going to find even a second Katharine P, and her doubtfully acknowledged belief that even if she did it would be a bad situation, has filled her with a sort of emotional lassitude as far as her lesbian friends are concerned. Since what she wants, what she feels she needs, is almost certainly unobtainable and definitely undesirable, Mary is careless about her lesbian relationships. They have become almost exclusively reduced to a sexual level. She enjoys the sense of conquest, refuses to make any emotional effort to establish a stable relationship, and quickly tires once the novelty of the situation has worn off. Since there is no chance of getting what she wants, she tends to shrug and think, "Why not?"

Significantly, Mary's father played a very shadowy and inconclusive role in her life. She seldom talks about him and certainly is not particularly interested in him. Whether this is a result of his own personality or, as is much more probable, because he was crowded out of Mary's life by her fantasies of a mother, it is difficult to say. But men are not impressive creatures as far as Mary is concerned. She is physically attracted to them, has a very positive physical response to their looks and bodies, but otherwise they do not particularly interest her. She enjoys their attentions, and is sexually warm towards them. But she gives the impression of never really taking them seriously. She never seems to consider them as prospective husbands, as someone with whom she could share her life to advantage. On the surface, Mary has taken refuge in received attitudes based on her experience with the young Frenchman she thought she loved. Thus she declares that all men are only interested in one thing, incapable of forming a lasting emotional relationship. In actual fact, Mary is an innocent about men. Emotionally they frighten her, and the fact that she feels instinctively drawn to women for emotional fulfilment means that intellectually she refuses to take them seriously. Women modelled on Katharine P are her intellectual heroines, and no man can rival them. Consequently, this denial of a respect and consideration which most men take for granted often succeeds in undermining any relationship Mary forms with a member of the opposite sex. She can cope happily on the sexual level, is a practised lover, but this expertise cloaks a fundamental lack of self-confidence in her attitude towards men that successfully prevents her forming any close relationship with them. The future looks bleak for Mary F, for it can only be a matter of time before the refuge of her careless, shoulder-shrugging attitude crumbles to reveal the stark truth of her emotional loneliness.

All too often, the bisexual woman follows the broad pattern of Mary F. The clue to their behaviour is always a search for some ideal and, sadly, such women are seldom able to settle for less, even when, like Mary, they recognise the futility and unwisdom of their search. Usually this need is accompanied by an emotional immaturity which is also instrumental in their failure to form a satisfying relationship. Such women, as it happens, are not obviously immature. On the contrary, they are likely to present themselves as mature, sophisticated creatures, and sexually, so they are. But this is only because their search has inevitably given them a lot of sexual experience and confidence. They have stressed their sexual expertise as a refuge from their emotional dissatisfaction. Such women, then, although highly proficient lovers, are emotionally unstable. They demand far more than they can possibly give or have any right to expect. They never allow themselves to be emotionally giving because they are so preoccupied with their own need for demonstrations of affection and for reassurances. This is why they flit so easily from sex to sex. The failure is never theirs, but always the bewildered partner's. So when a man "fails", they turn to a woman, and when that relationship does not supply what they need, they blame it on the irregularity of the liaison and turn to some new man to try again, only to fail again. As this process continues, so the importance of sex becomes overblown. Eventually there is a danger of sexual acts being used as substitutes for proper relationships, with the result that the affairs become shorter and shorter and proportionately more frustrating.

The pathetic history of Milly E is also indicative of a type of bisexual woman who is by no means uncommon. However, because of her circumstances, Milly is a somewhat extreme case, as is illustrated by her profession. Milly is a prostitute. At sixteen, she must have been a very attractive girl. Naturally blonde, small, with a sharp, intelligent face, Milly is the sort of girl who seems to have been built to turn men's heads and, like so many of her kind, she also seems to be disastrously unable to repulse the advances made to her. Consequently, before she was seventeen, Milly had experienced a painful, self-induced abortion. By eighteen, she was on the streets and keeping a man out of the proceeds. This was Milly's first, and probably last, experience of loving a man.

"Oh, I was a fool," Milly says wryly when she speaks of the affair. "We ran away together, up to the smoke. He was twenty-five, I was eighteen. It was going to be love in a garret. Make our fortunes. Only he didn't get a job, did he? Oh, I'm not saying he didn't try. He did, at first. But then he got to like not working and that was my lot. He put me out. I had to wear dark glasses for the first week to cover the black eye he gave me. Yes, he beat me up when I wouldn't do it.

"Why did I stay with him? I don't know, because he was smashing, I suppose. Tall, dark and good-looking, you know. He was what I thought a man should be. When he wanted to, he could make me feel like a queen, but God help you once you got across him. And he was marvellous in bed. I should know, and you can take it from me he really was fantastic. When you come to think about it, I would have done anything to have him lying on top of me. And do you know, when they done him on a list of charges as long as my arm, I cried my bleeding eyes out. He was a real swine, there's no two ways about it, but I thought the world of him. I could go on and on forgiving him. I learnt not to mind the clients."

With her exploiter and protector safely behind bars, Milly did not know what to do. She received a helping hand from a more experienced woman, Cora, and the two girls set up home and business together. In this way they were able to handle their own business and avoid the clutches of the pimps.

"Me and Cora got on all right. She put me wise to a lot and it was nice having company. Cora and me, we'd been through the same sort of thing, and that sort of made a bond between us. And we both did pretty well. We did the flat up nice, ate well and put a bit by. Then one day Cora comes in and she wants to know if I'm game to make fifty quid. I told her she must be daft to ask, but she says, 'Hold on a minute. It's for something special.' She didn't want to get me involved unless I was really willing to go through with it. And you know what it was? Lesbians. That's what. Some bloke had offered a hundred quid for Cora to put on a lesbian show with another girl for him and a few friends.

"Well, I didn't know what to say. I mean, I didn't know anything about it, did I? So I asked Cora and she said she'd done it once or twice before and she could easily get another girl if I didn't want to. Well, that got the old pride going, didn't it? If Cora could do it, so could I. Anyway, I was greedy for that fifty. So I said I'd do it, and Cora explained it all to me. You know, it sounded silly to me, then. Women going at each other. It seemed daft. And another thing, Cora wanted to have a rehearsal, but I wouldn't. I said I'd be all right on the night. I just couldn't bring myself to do it somehow, not without a proper reason.

"Well, we went along to this bloke's house, somewhere out in the suburbs it was. We got undressed in this little room, then we went out to where all these fellows were, having this party. 'Course they all started cheering and shouting when they saw us, but old Cora just grabbed hold of my tits and started kissing me and they soon shut up. And you know what? I really got excited. I didn't have to act. Old Cora really knew what she was doing and soon I was ready to come off. I just did whatever she did, and I was so hot and bothered I didn't have time to feel funny about it. I was having too much of a good time myself. Well, then we got to the sucking bit and that really did it. I went wild. I was thrashing and writhing and moaning all over the place, and before you could say Jack Robinson, I'd spun round and was sixty-nining with Cora.

"Honestly, it was better than my bloke, you know, the one I told you about. I'd never had sex like it. I was in a daze when we'd finished, and some bloke jumped on top of me and I couldn't have cared less. I was right up there on cloud seven, and nothing could bring me down.

"Well, when we got back, it must have been almost dawn, old Cora puts her arm round me and she says, 'You really liked it, didn't you?' I had to say 'yes', didn't I? And we did it again. Afterwards, Cora told me she was a real dyke, and we've been together ever since. I've never been with a man except for money since, and I won't do the lesbian bit in public. Even though it's well paid. Cora would, but I won't let her. You see, that's between me and her. I'll take on twenty blokes in front of an audience, but not the other. That's private. That's my life now.

"I still live with Cora and I hope I always will. We're very cosy, just like man and wife really. We take our holidays together, have the odd day off to enjoy ourselves. We even share blokes sometimes when one of them wants to team up. No, I don't think I love Cora, certainly not in the way I loved that bloke. Nothing like that could ever happen to me again. But Cora was good to me when I needed help, and she's always been good. And she never laid a finger on me against my will. Afterwards, she told me how much she wanted to but how she restrained herself. I think that's marvellous. It shows that she really thought about *me*, and not many people have ever bothered to do that. But Cora's like that, and she's completely dependable. If she says she's going to do something, you know she will. Not like blokes. They're all talk and no action. And then there's the sex. That's best of all. After a day flopping on your back for a lot of selfish men, you can't know the relief it is to climb into bed with Cora and know that someone's going to make *love* to you, not just use your body for themselves. And she makes love to *me*. I always come off with Cora, two or three times, but never with a bloke. It's not a hard life, I suppose, but the good things in it are all Cora's doing."

When asked to elaborate on her early life, Milly told of a broken home, an unsupervised childhood and all the misery that so often results from such situations. Milly's early experiences obviously hardened her to the world, but this hardness cloaked the usual romanticism that is so much a part not only of the young girl, but frequently of the bisexual woman. Thus she was almost certain to be swept off her feet by the first likely man who came along, and whereas another girl would have thought twice before setting off for London with a young man without prospects, Milly never questioned his promises. As in everything else, in the complete absence of guidance, Milly had to learn the hard way.

We see at once that the root of her behaviour and of her problem, if such we may term it, is her lack of security. Milly had never known a stable home. Right from her childhood she had had to learn to be independent, and this entailed dealing with her own mistakes. To such a girl, any promise of a better life is almost pathetically believable. And unlike better equipped girls, Milly could not see her flight to London as a risk. After all, she was only exchanging one form of insecurity for another, and the risk, particularly in the company of an attractive and desirable young man, seemed well worth taking.

Her enduring love for the man, which was undoubtedly genuine, despite his appalling treatment of her, is also a mark of her insecurity. In Milly's ramshackle world, it is always a case of better the devil you know. She clung to him because he was the only permanent fixture in a changing, bewildering world. In this connection, it is revealing that the only time Milly admits to being completely at a loss was when the man was arrested, tried and sentenced. Then there was no one. Even being forced to walk the streets, to submit to the caresses of paying clients, to risk a beating were bearable because she always had the man to return to. He was *hers*, and she belonged to him. In a tenuous world, Milly's only sense of her own identity comes directly from those who love her, or whom she believes love her.

Thus Cora appears at once as a saviour. Her treatment of Milly throughout their relationship is obviously unselfish and genuinely kind. To Milly this must have seemed absolutely extraordinary. The discovery of her ability to enjoy lesbian practices completed an already well founded relationship. Cora became the permanent fixture, the point of reference. For the first time, with Cora, Milly was able to build her own home. She could depend upon Cora, Cora bothered about her and did not try to exploit her. Above all, Cora could satisfy her physically where men, by reason of their very familiarity and frequency, could not.

We learn most about Milly's relationship with Cora from her fiercely possessive attitude towards it. She makes it clear that Cora is above criticism, and harps upon her generosity, *e.g.* the fact that she did not seduce Milly even though she wanted to. But it is her refusal to perform in lesbian spectacles and her preventing Cora from doing so that most clearly indicates the importance of the affair to Milly. It is something private, something personal. It is, in fact, the love of her life, and she reacts as any normal woman would if asked to make love to her husband before an audience. Such relationships are powerful simply because they are virtually sacred. Finally, in her insistence on the fact that Cora is concerned with *her*, we see positive proof of her insecurity and lack of identity. With Cora she is safe from exploitation. This is the one relationship in her life in which the other person does consider her as an equal human being and not as a means to an end. Love is very often based upon this identity confirmation, and to one as unsettled and insecure as Milly, it has a very special importance indeed.

Because of her way of life and her experiences with the man who first made her become a prostitute, Milly is, not surprisingly, sceptical about men. Her own carelessness with her body, her pathetically trusting nature and now her years of brutal experience have planted a fundamental mistrust of men in her mind. She lives by necessity in a world where men are accepted as being selfish, out to exploit a woman's body for pleasure or gain without much, if any, thought of the woman as a complete personality. Only Cora has treated her as she needs to be treated. Only Cora has been concerned with Milly's pleasure, Milly's happiness. And over the years, Cora has remained. She is the exception which proves the rule about men. It is extremely unlikely that Milly will ever permit herself to trust another man, especially since her relationship with Cora is so satisfying that she does not feel the need.

Sexually, Milly has no problems. She is quite happily adjusted to her homosexuality and thinks of herself as perfectly normal. Heterosexuality she regards as intermittently pleasurable, but it does not compare with the pleasure she gets with Cora. It is first and foremost her work and as such she takes little interest in it. She calmly accepted the suggestion that she was bisexual, but made it quite clear that such labels have little meaning for her.

Insecurity is frequently an influential factor in bisexual

behaviour, both for men and women. The lack of security which frequently almost becomes the norm, is still instinctively rejected. Often it spills over into the question of personal identity, as it did in the case of Milly E. Such a person is motivated, sexually and emotionally, by two needs. Firstly, they need to put down roots, to feel that there is something dependable in the world, and secondly, to have their identity affirmed. So often they have been forced to cultivate their independence to such an extent that they can no longer be sure that they have any effect on other people, especially if, as so frequently happens, others regard them as mere pawns to be used at will. These needs are very effective inhibition removers, for the quest for assurance and permanence over-rides all normal objections. This is strengthened, in the majority of cases, by the fact that such people have often lead morally loose lives and have, almost naturally, fewer inhibitions than their more fortunate brothers and sisters.

Because of this history of insecurity which characterises such cases and largely motivates them, they do not, like so many bisexuals, instinctively seek to destroy the permanence they want. The gap in their lives is very real. They are not seeking to replace or substitute something, but to find something they never had. Thus when, like Milly, they find a partner who makes them feel real, who provides them with a measure of security, they generally react favourably. They defend and protect this state, are loyal, dependable and deeply grateful to the lover who has, to all intents and purposes, provided them with a place in the world. It is not uncommon for such people to be temporary bisexuals. By this we mean that once they have found what they need, they can abandon their bisexuality. This is particularly true of women in this situation who often make excellent, faithful wives, or become fiercely loyal lesbians. But for the others, their bisexual urge acts as a constant threat to the security they have so painfully won. They generally try to be loyal, to be unisexual in their behaviour, but they do not always succeed. Curiously, this is because although they have achieved a measure of physical security, they need to be constantly reaffirmed as to their identity. Thus their sexual adventures, often with people of the opposite sex to their permanent partner, is an attempt to gain this reassurance fleetingly but over and over again.

Vivienne C on the other hand, enjoyed all the advantages that were sadly lacking in Milly E's youth. A secure home, doting parents, an excellent education and a reasonable degree of affluence. These attractions, however, were the prime constituents of boredom as far as Vivienne was concerned. This solid family was built upon a scrupulous concern with the Church which Vivienne and her brothers were forced to attend, and although they lacked for nothing, the threat of God's eternal punishment was continually held over them. Vivienne rebelled against this, to her, arbitrary series of rules and her rebellion extended to a vehement despising of all the solid middle-class virtues which her parents both represented and extolled.

"It was strictly dullsville," she said, with a deliberate steely "flip" manner which she has adopted as a virtual symbol of her dissatisfaction with her background. "God, you've no idea how dull it was, or rather is, I should say. I mean, when you freak out in the hope of injecting a little life into them, all they do is say God will punish you, be careful, think what you're doing. It really gives me the icks."

Once she discovered, with all the confidence of the modern teenager, that God did not punish her here and now, Vivienne's rebellion seethed to the surface. Her long suffering parents continually refused to rise to the bait and this unwittingly added to their headstrong daughter's anger. She proudly announced that she had lost her virginity, but the storm she expected would greet this news was not forthcoming. "Daddy prayed and Mummy wept," she said contemptuously, "and then they both went and talked it over with the Vicar. It was a great scene."

Finally, because her parents equated the theatrical world with some contemporary hell, and because there was nothing else she wished to do, Vivienne joined a nearby theatrical company as an assistant stage manager.

"All this time I'd been screwing around and I'd got to like it," she said. "You know, I even contemplated getting pregnant, but I couldn't face it and was always very careful. Anyway, since the parents couldn't face up to having a loose moraled daughter, I thought joining the theatre would get the message over. They were shocked, humiliated and ashamed, or so they said. But that was all.

"So, there I was, all set for a glittering theatrical career and fully prepared to enjoy my first taste of freedom. But what a sell! All the guys were either too old, too scared or queer. Honestly, you've never seen so many gay guys in one place in your entire life. So I joined the club. I shacked up with this cool dark chick, Estelle. She was always the lady who did it, or 'Rebecca'. And she was the biggest dyke in the whole world. I mean it. It was really a gas the way she went about bringing me out. I was so screwed up, I'd have done anything to get an orgasm, but Estelle had to play this great soul-searching scene. It was all beautifully sinful darling, but this thing is bigger than both of us.

"Well, surprise, surprise. I liked it. And knew it was forbidden. For the first time in my life I felt good, really good. I'd done something people really got uptight about. I'd made a prohibited scene and soon I was the biggest dyke in the business. No girl was safe from me. I shaved my hair and bought a butch shirt. It was wild. In no time at all I had a reputation as a fearless lesbian, a peril to all young girls."

Not surprisingly, Vivienne lost her job. She moved to

London and again using her lesbianism as a sort of identity, became assistant stage manager to a commercial company, working on various West End presentations. In this job she was successfully challenged by a young man who broke the myth of her lesbianism in the most obvious and convincing way.

"I realised I was bisexual," said Vivienne, with an unmistakeable note of pride. "A swinger both ways, that's me. A pretty girl, a nice guy, who cares? Its all the same to me. You know, I've even had both together, and two guys at once? Man, that was a real happening!"

Vivienne C is so entrenched in her own fantasy world that it is impossible to get any factual information from her. She is concerned to impress and does so by spinning a web of words which she imagines presents her as the arch-fiend of bisexuality. Any attempt to penetrate the myth she offers makes her hostile and reticent. Genuinely factual information she regards as boring and unimportant. She wants to get back to her exploits and to prove to one how shocking, immoral and worthless she is.

Because of her upbringing, Vivienne C has decided that anything "forbidden", *i.e.* not condoned and approved by her parents' strict and admittedly unimaginative moral code, is automatically glamorous and worthy. She is a high-spirited, nervous and sensitive girl. Her reactions to the intellectual dullness and confining moral stringency of her home life is perfectly natural and comprehensible. It is a slightly dramatised form of the rebellion which is essential to virtually all young people. They kick against what is nearest, irrespective of its true merits and disadvantages, in order to prove their identity, to demonstrate their independence. But even though she admittedly has a valid cause for rejecting her parents' way of life, her way of doing so is still ludicrously exaggerated. Despite all the fuss and noise, Vivienne is more truly a product of her background and more firmly still in the grip of her parents than either of her brothers, whose quiet conformity but true independence she regards as a betrayal.

During their childhood and adolescence, both brothers were more subtle in their forms of revolt. As a result, it was Vivienne who stood out. Her deliberately provocative behaviour caused her to be punished and lectured more often and more strictly than her brothers. Undoubtedly, she felt that this meant that her parents did not love her as much as the boys. Since then, her behaviour, her deliberate attempts to shock and hurt, are an attempt to punish her parents for this supposed failure, and also to keep their attention firmly on her. Significantly, her calculated loss of virginity and the ritual announcement of the fact occurred at the same time as the news of her elder brother's having won a scholarship to Oxford. This fact greatly pleased the parents who made a fuss of the boy which seemed to detract from their attention to Vivienne. This attention, this love, she desperately needs.

Her lesbianism, although it is probably true that it was occasioned by a lack of willing male partners in the first place, is also a part of her rebellion. Not only does she hope to shock and hurt her parents, but she also defies the God whose punishment she still half expects. By adopting so readily and so arbitrarily the *persona* of a case-book lesbian, Vivienne felt that she had successfully cut herself off from her family. This separated her from them, yet the moment she had cut her hair and adopted mannish clothing, she visited her parents in order to parade this new image before them.

Because she feels unloved, unnoticed, the attributes of lesbianism also gave her a sort of ready-made identity. It attracted attention, and she fed off the shock and speculation that her appearance and manner inevitably produced. Therefore, when a young man challenged this pose and demonstrated her heterosexual propensities once again, not only was Vivienne's view of herself punctured, but her punishment of her parents was nullified. Hence the wholehearted, enthusiastic adoption of bisexuality. This, in her mind, is a worse sexual sin than mere lesbianism. To be both, to be an indiscriminate sexual pleasure seeker is the most wicked, *i.e.* most glamorous and interesting, *persona* she can achieve. She boasts of her exploits and makes periodic returns to her family, accompanied by a retinue of sexual partners. Although she cannot accept this, Vivienne hopes always to be forgiven for her transgressions, to be exonerated and taken again to the bosom of the family she vilifies.

Beneath this complicated family involvement, of course, Vivienne C's bisexuality is a classic search for love. But she will not find it until she has reconciled her ambivalent attitudes towards her parents. Their approval, their love is the salve which will heal the wounds she continually inflicts upon herself. But because of her ingrained religious response, this love must be given in the form of forgiveness for her sins. She must be washed clean by her parents' compassionate tears, and only then will she be able to come to terms with herself and with life.

Once again, Vivienne's problem is indicative of a common bisexual situation. The equation of the disapproved with the attractive is all too common, and the bisexual often dramatises his or her nature for this very reason. Inevitably, there are other motives and more often than not these are concerned with punishment, both of the self and of others. Punishment and forgiveness, love and attention are craved by many bisexuals who exploit their dual sexual natures for these ends. All too frequently, it is a fruitless search, and since the needs are so conflicting, so great, this type of bisexual is invariably neurotic, undependable and given to violent acts of self-destruction. Sadly, their sexual propensities increase the fundamentally unbearable feeling that they do not belong completely to any one world, either that of conformity or of rebellion.

They are spiritually placeless, rootless creatures who, as usual, use sex not only as a substitute for love but as a weapon against the world that has apparently rejected them.

Here then are three common types of bisexual behaviour and motivation which are particularly relevant to women. Bisexual men, of course, do evince identical symptoms and behaviour patterns, often for the same motives, but, by and large, most individuals who fall into these categories are women. Each type is in a sad predicament and there is seldom much help that can usefully be given. Their lives have been blighted and their bisexuality is no more than a symptom of a condition. Very often the small measure of happiness they achieve is a direct result of their sexual tastes, but it is, unfortunately, inevitably a perversion of the true nature of sexuality. Most disturbing of all is the fact that society's attitude to homosexuality often encourages the bisexual to use half of his sexual urge as a weapon which, not surprisingly, only adds to his or her natural confusion. It is a vicious circle which, hopefully, will be abolished as society learns to adopt a more tolerant attitude to personal sexual behaviour. When sex is used as a protest, it is inevitably unfulfilling and quickly becomes vulgarised. It ceases to be a panacea, a source of joy and only adds to a dilemma that is already sufficient cause in itself for concern.

CHAPTER 5: THE BISEXUAL MAN

The male bisexual differs from the female primarily in his attitudes to his own nature. We are speaking, of course, in very general terms for it is undoubtedly true that many bisexual men are as concerned with identity problems and lack of love as women, but the fact remains that their attitude to these problems and even their awareness of them is quite different. It is because the bisexual male is naturally better equipped to cope with the demands of his sexual urge that he often appears to be more successful and generally better integrated than women. In fact, this success is frequently no more than an illusion. All we are really saying is that his exterior presentation of the problem, of his very condition is more opaque and, conversely, the disturbing impulses which often motivate his behaviour are more deeply hidden.

Both natural and social factors, however, make it in many ways easier for a man to be a bisexual. Men are by nature more overtly sexual creatures. In the light of present day discoveries and beliefs, it is no longer possible to assert that the male in general has a stronger sexual urge than women. Certainly the object of sexual activity, its attendant circumstances and its general meaning are quite different for a man and for a woman. Their approach to sexual activity is indicative of their very sex, and we should never forget that bisexuals are, in these terms, completely masculine or completely feminine in their approaches. Furthermore, even the discovery of reliable contraception does not completely free a woman from her natural tendency to associate sexual intercourse with the prolonged processes of pregnancy and motherhood. But, simply because of the male's natural aggressive role, it appears that men are more strongly sexed than women. As we know, a whole mythology of sexual attitudes and beliefs has been erected on this apparent factor, and even in these enlightened days old beliefs die hard. Thus, socially, a man is expected to be overtly sexual, he is expected to "sow his wild oats" in a way which is not extended to women. A man who does not appear to be happily involved in some sexual liaison is regarded as something of an oddity, while for a girl a state of prolonged virginity is not only accepted but even encouraged. However, there is a qualitative difference between the imperious demands of the erect penis and the quiet longings of the vagina. Not only is the latter much easier to control, but total satisfaction is much harder to achieve. Total as the demands of the aroused penis are, they are also easily met and perhaps this factor alone explains much of the difference between the male and the female attitudes to sexual activity. The whole process is simpler for men. There is no possibility of after effects comparable to pregnancy. The very speed and ease of the activity makes it less important. Sex, to a man, is an end in itself, but to the majority of women it is a small part of a complex emotional, psychological and biological process.

Thus it is comparatively easy for a man's bisexuality to be seen as a simple matter of increased opportunity for sexual release. A woman, even if her sexual urge is very strong and drastically simplified, as is often the case among bisexuals, is still aware of a need for love and security. She cannot, even by the most gigantic effort of will, often ignore the question of love entirely. This is, therefore, the root of much of the female bisexual's dissatisfaction and fear. For a man, sexual intercourse of any kind can easily be regarded as an advanced, more satisfying form of masturbation. It need not necessarily have the intense emotional significance that invariably dogs a woman. On the contrary, the young man is often anxiously concerned to avoid the responsibilities sex places upon him. His dilemma arises out of the often conflicting needs of his body and his female partner. So, in its most simple terms, the bisexual man has a basic attitude to sex which better equips him to cope with the duality of his sexual nature. The physical act is of prime importance, not its emotional connotations. Sex, for him, is not the symbol of love and trust it is to woman, and so the fact that he sleeps contentedly with both men and women does not necessarily disturb him since there is no emotional involvement, but a simple sharing of sexual pleasure which is sufficient in itself.

The problem arises, of course, from the general attitudes to male homosexuality. As we have already said, male homosexuality, even today, is widely regarded as infinitely more reprehensible than lesbianism. Until recently it was punishable by law, even in this country, and there are still many governments who condemn the practice. We can understand something of this disparate and apparently illogical attitude if we consider homosexuality and lesbianism at their most fundamental levels. Not only do they go against the teachings of the church since they are prime examples of sex being used for carnal non-procreative ends, but they may also be regarded as activities which symbolise the human concern with sexual pleasure. Simply because the male has always been regarded as an aggressive, even insatiable sexual creature, homosexuality has been forbidden. It seems to many to be the very last straw, an example of the male perverting Nature because of his overweening sexual desire. Although society successfully restricted his heterosexual outlets, they would not tolerate this other means of obtaining pleasure. They would turn a blind eye to wild oat sowing, to brothels and mistresses, even in the strictest times, but homosexuality was going too far and was therefore officially outlawed. Why not lesbianism too? Simply because women were regarded as disinterested, asexual creatures. Lesbianism was unthinkable, even though evidence of it abounded. And furthermore, of course, since the law makers are inevitably men, they could afford to tolerate lesbianism because it constituted no threat to them personally. The exclusive heterosexual male has always had such an exaggerated fear of homosexuality that without the protection of repressive laws, he has never felt safe from his deviated brethren.

In some ways, we must expect the bisexual man to inherit some of these attitudes. He often fears homosexuality as much as the heterosexual male. And since he is invariably accepted as a heterosexual, he stands to lose much more than the confirmed homosexual, who has no choice in the matter, by his sexual allegiance to his own kind. Even if his own homosexual instincts are so strong as to render his own objections ineffectual, those of society and often particularly of woman whom he also desires, create a genuine problem, act as a true source of fear. Indeed it is possible to regard the "success" of the bisexual male solely in terms of his ability to accept and cope with the "stigma" of his homosexuality. Very few men achieve this completely, but there are a number of excuses and justifications in which they believe and which satisfactorily place them, in their own opinion, above reproach. These subterfuges, as we shall endeavour to show, are often the most revealing aspects of the male bisexual who is, however, nearly always characterised by an extrovert approach which is the most immediately striking, though not necessarily the most fundamental, difference between him and his bisexual sister.

Alan H, for example, is a youth in his late teens who experiences a by no means unnatural powerful sexual urge. He regards himself as unduly highly sexed, although he will, in all probability, find that the sexual storms of late adolescence will abate to more manageable proportions if, that is, Alan himself will give them a chance. Alan comes from a large but comfortably off family and his dual concerns, at present, are his ambitions and his sexual needs. He is determined to become a successful physicist, and his family are bent on helping him. This fact is so important to him because Alan is the only one of six children who has so far shown any signs of academic brilliance. This factor at once distinguishes him from the rest of the family and makes him more determined to try. The one threat to his success is his sexual urge, or so he sees it. This is based on the fact that at fifteen he made a girl pregnant. His sexual precocity badly affected his standing in the home, and his irate father lectured him on the perils of putting sexual satisfaction, at best a fleeting pleasure, before scholastic achievement.

"I was clearly given to understand," says Alan H ruefully, "that if it happened again after I was sixteen, the family would not support me. I'd have to fend for myself, marry the girl and give up all ideas of university. I saw the family's point of view, and I think they behaved correctly. Though there was no need to make that amount of fuss about it. Anyway, I listened and took notice. But I knew it was going to be damned difficult. You see, most of the girls who'll let you don't have any idea about contraception and I can't bear using a rubber. I have done, on occasions, but it's never the same. It doesn't feel the same, and the whole business makes me feel sick. I like the feeling of flesh in flesh, not to have it separated by a rubber sheath."

The answer to Alan's problem, which became acute when he heard stories of the unreliability of male contraceptives, was homosexuality.

"I went away one summer with a group of friends, and there were three of us in this one tent and we just started fooling around when we were undressing. You know, grabbing at each other, that sort of thing. Well, we all got pretty excited, and I was wrestling with this one boy and I touched his bottom, sort of up in between, you know. I could tell at once that he liked it, so later that night, I went over to him and I put my penis up him. He said it hurt a bit, but he liked it. I think he was queer because he really liked it. It felt great to me too. Tighter than a girl and absolutely no danger. It might never have gone any further than that but for the fact that I discovered how easy it is to find boys who'll let you do that to them. Much easier than girls. Young boys, about fourteen or so, are always dying to know about sex and everything, and it's easy to persuade them. Older guys, too, are often a pushover and the world is full of old blokes who will let you do it or who are longing to suck you off."

Alan H insists that he is absolutely heterosexual, that he despises homosexuals and that his behaviour with young boys is perfectly blameless. He plans to marry in due course, and there will be, he assures himself, an immediate end to his homosexual practices. He only ever takes the active role, and he regards the whole sordid process as an acceptable substitute for masturbation and heterosexual intercourse. He has no interest in his male partners other than as a source of sexual relief. Girls are his ultimate goal, but his sexual relations with them are limited now to heavy petting and caressing. This is, he says, not enough, and hence his homosexual activities. They are born and executed of necessity, and are only a temporary measure. Time alone will tell whether Alan H's assessment of the situation is accurate. Possibly it is, but his brutal, selfish and quite amoral attitude seems unlikely to make him a loyal, satisfied husband and there is no reason to suppose that his attraction to his own sex does not go much more deeply than he allows himself to admit.

Alan H's bisexuality is not a symptom of his general

situation, but a natural off-shoot of it. He has a very high opinion of himself. In the company of girls he swaggers and promotes his masculinity quite deliberately. His intellectual superiority to his brothers and sisters is the root cause of this attitude. It sets him apart within the family, makes him special. The other children have had to adapt to him and his achievements have been used as an example to them. His sexual precocity is not unusual in itself, nor is it as powerful as he would have one believe. If it were, his adherence to his father's advice would not be so slavish. What matters to him is his parents' good opinion. His escapade with the girl seriously detracted from the esteem in which he was held, and if he were really the sensible, super-intelligent boy he likes to seem, he would have found celibacy no more difficult than other boys of his age. But his sexual prowess is the secret of his popularity with his contemporaries. What academic achievement does for him at home, sexual adventurousness does for him among his peers who have a healthy scorn for schoolwork. He avoids being regarded as a dull swot by being a sexual deviate. His homosexuality is undoubtedly not mere expedience. There must be a genuine attraction and enjoyment for him in these activities. He boasts of them, but secretly he knows that they would damage his image in his parents' eyes more strongly than his heterosexual activities. For this reason he is brutal with his male partners. He seduces young boys he can intimidate. He is a sexual bully, ashamed of his own propensities, frightened that some boy will one day reveal this unsavoury aspect of his personality. In short, Alan H lives in a myth of his own importance and separateness. He has become accustomed to being "different" from his brothers and sisters, and this need to perpetuate his "differentness" is reflected by his homosexuality. Not only does it make him "important", but also sets him apart from others as well as giving him an opportunity to exercise his "power" over others.

His reluctance to have intercourse with girls, although very logically rationalised, is unconvincing and one cannot but suspect that his homosexuality is much stronger than his heterosexual urge. If he persists in this way, he undoubtedly stands to face a number of damaging problems in the future, particularly if, as he claims, he attempts to make an unqualified transfer to girls as sexual partners. Some unavoidable evidence of failure is required to bring perspective into his life, but unfortunately, such failure is almost certain to feed the fires of his sexual activities with harmful results.

Another very interesting case, and one that is typical of the bisexual's ambivalent attitude to his own situation, is that of Martin B. In his early thirties, Martin has a very successful job, but is not married. He is, however, never short of attractive girl friends, many of whom share his bed. He is also frequently to be seen in exclusively homosexual bars and clubs, and often leaves these establishments with a male partner. He is undeniably bisexual, but utterly refuses to accept this.

"I adore girls. I prefer making love to an attractive girl to anything. I am completely normal. The sensation of penetrating a girl, of all that soft warm flesh gripping your manhood is absolutely unbeatable. I'd spend my life in bed with a girl if I could. As it is, I spend a hell of a lot of time there.

"When I pick up a man, it's purely for certain sensations. It's simple necessity. It doesn't make me queer. I love to be fellated, and very few girls will do that. Even when they do they're not much good at it, and I don't like having to instruct them. Anyone will tell you that homos are best at sucking. They've had more practice and it gives them a thrill as well. I never do anything else. I always pick someone who likes to do it, and then we go somewhere and I let him suck me to orgasm. The sensations of a practised tongue around the *glans* is unbeatable, and when the fellator swallows it, it is indescribable. I admit I get a curious kind of thrill, too, from ejaculating in their throats. I have never done that to a girl, but queers like it.

"Yes, I do all this and I like it, but it does not make me queer. It's just a variation. For me, it's the equivalent of going to a brothel. You don't think other men are abnormal because they visit brothels, do you?"

This very truculent statement, full of sweeping generalities and protestations of sexual normalcy, is quite transparent. Martin B is a classic example of an unresolved bisexual, and his pathetic justification is typical of the behaviour of many bisexuals who share a similar problem. One such declared that he enjoyed passive anal intercourse, that it gave him a special pleasure but that he hated any suggestion of homosexual behaviour! By limiting the range of their activities in homosexual situations, many bisexual men turn themselves into near fetishists, with the activity replacing the object. This generally exonerates them, as far as they are concerned, from any suggestion of *their* homosexuality. In Martin B's case, his reasoning is more than usually unconvincing. Today very few women will refuse to perform fellatio on their lovers since oral sex has become an established and accepted forerunner to sexual intercourse itself. It is certain that Martin B does not ask his female partners to perform this service for him and even when they do he obviously feels uncomfortable in the situation.

Like James W whose case we examined earlier in this book, Martin B is unsure of women and has an unrealistic fear of desecrating them. This stems, in his case, from a saintly mother, a woman of vaunted goodness and exaggerated gentility who exerts, even today, a considerable influence on her son. From her, Martin has inherited a false view of women. As he has grown older, the full-blooded heterosexual man in him has seen that marriage to such a creature as he imagines women to be is, to say the least, undesirable. Thus, although he has overcome his received scruples about having intercourse with girls outside marriage, he has carefully avoided marriage itself. And simply because, deep down, he regards women as saintly, inviolable creatures, he feels unable to indulge in oral acts with them. Not surprisingly, Martin B irrationally equates oral sex with dirty, prohibited behaviour. Thus, although drawn to his own sex, he limits his activities to passive fellation. By so doing, by allowing a despised homosexual to perform a "dirty" act on him, he denigrates those members of his own sex and "protects" himself from any taint of being like them. With typical ambivalence, he equates ejaculation into the mouth of his partner with their debasement and his superiority.

Were it not for his unacknowledged attraction to his own sex, Martin B's craving for fellatio, implanted in him by an older cousin when he was a small pubescent boy, would easily have been satisfied by his female partners. However, his feelings about the opposite sex and about homosexuality prohibit this, and simultaneously justify his own indulgence in homosexual acts. Further probing revealed a desire on his part to play a more active role in homosexual situations, and a fear that these liaisons would threaten and perhaps destroy any meaningful relationship he might manage to establish with a girl. Only when he has resolved, one way or the other, his fears about homosexuality can he hope to achieve a satisfactory heterosexual relationship.

It is a common error for bisexual men to claim that a certain kind of pleasure can only be obtained with their own sex, although, except for very obvious examples, this is by no means true. The addiction to the act, which they claim to be unable to forego, is used to hide their basic attraction to their own sex. The fact that this activity, *e.g.* fellatio, anal intercourse, can only be obtained with men, although this is not true, is a matter beyond their control.

Their liking for the act therefore necessitates their participation, they claim, but does not make them homosexual. Invariably, these acts are regarded, by the bisexual, as a denigration of the partner which also serves to salve the bisexual's conscience.

Carried to its logical conclusion, this form of sexual attitude ambivalence can result in examples of the most disturbed bisexual behaviour. Such an example, and it is not a pleasant one, is provided by the case of Colin L who occupied an apparently normal environment. On the surface, Colin L was like hundreds of other young men. He had a good job, a number of girl friends, and shared a flat with another young man. But in all these apparently normal activities and situations, something was jarringly wrong. His job, although it offered good prospects within an established organisation, was one he professed to hate. The promotion that should have been inevitable had passed him by, largely because he made the minimum of effort while assuring that his behaviour and attitudes never became so bad that he was sacked. He made no attempt to find another job. His girl friends, on the other hand, changed with amazing rapidity. Few girls slept with him more than once. He treated them badly and seemed to delight in reducing them to tears. On occasions he struck them. During the course of enquiries, a number of girls volunteered the information that he was sadistically cruel, that he forced them to perform acts which distressed them and used them roughly. Finally, the apparently simple and innocent situation of sharing a flat with another young man was revealed to be extremely questionable. The flat-mate was, in fact, a confirmed passive homosexual who acted not only as a periodic bed mate, but as a combined housekeeper and sexual slave as well.

Colin L admitted to being bisexual and aggressively added, "Anyone who isn't, is a fool. Sex is paramount today. At last we're losing our inhibitions and hang ups and are beginning to admit that we like sex, that sex is where it's at. Once you've done that, how can you confine yourself to one form of sexual expression or to one person? Sex is an adventure, and the bisexuals are the only ones who really know this. To be exclusively hetero is just to put your head in the marriage trap, and a queer misses out all the way down the line. No, today, the only logical thing to do is to go both ways."

Not content with accepting his dual sexual nature, if, in fact, he does, Colin L has to make it a virtue. Bisexuality is the only proper way to live, and therefore we are meant to understand that his catholic sexual tastes make him a better, freer person. Of course this is not true, and when a man protests so much we can be certain that his protestations hide some deep-seated disturbance. More evidence of this disturbance was supplied by an ex-girl friend of Colin L's who said:

"I think he is very sick, but more to be pitied than blamed. I only went to bed with him once and he was impotent at first. This made him terribly angry, and after a while he said it was my fault. He did this great spiel about how women always assumed they only had to lay on their backs to excite a man but that this wasn't enough. He said if I knew anything about sex, I would know that I had to arouse him. I suppose I made matters worse because I said perhaps it was his bisexuality, perhaps I didn't really appeal to him. You see, he'd always made such a big thing of going with boys as well, I thought it was very important to him. And then when he couldn't, well, get hard with me, I thought maybe he was really queer and didn't like to let on. I only meant to be kind, but he was furious and said he'd show me what sort of man he was.

"He pushed me around a bit and then made me fellate him. I don't really mind doing that but it should be an expression of affection. I hated doing it because he made me. He pulled my hair, and just held my face there. It was horrible. It helped him a bit, though, but not much. Then he said I had to kiss and lick his bottom. He said all the boys did that and women should as well. I just couldn't. I mean it just disgusted me, and when I refused he hit me. I was frightened and started crying. I wanted to leave but he wouldn't let me. But while I was all upset, he got an erection and then he took me, savagely, and all the time he kept pinching my breasts and biting me hard and calling me names. It took him a long time, too, and it was awful. I never went with him again. He's terribly attractive and at first, when he got moody and unpleasant, I just thought it was because he was unhappy in his job and things got on top of him. But after that night, I guessed it went deeper than that, and I just steered clear of him. I knew I couldn't cope."

This testimony is widely at variance with Colin L's own picture of his heterosexual relationships.

"Women just flock to me. They love it. Women know a bisexual's a good screw. They know they'll get the whole bit. The trouble is, I'm so good at sex they fall in love with me. That's when I send them packing. Either that, or they can't stand the pace. But no bird leaves me for any other reason. Yes, I've slapped a girl around a bit occasionally. They like it. They're naturally submissive, born masochists. They like the sense of being dominated. They know they're with a real man then. And sometimes you have to persuade them to vary the routine a bit. Humiliation helps to fulfil a woman. It's just a game. Once they've blown me or let me sodomise them, they love it. It just takes a few slaps to overcome their inhibitions."

An extraordinary and very revealing attitude which, like so much that Colin L says, is transparently a rationalisation of the truth. His impotence, for example, is never referred to. Nor, significantly, was it mentioned by his flat-mate.

"Yes, he's very brutal, but that is part of his attraction as far as I am concerned. And he can also be very sweet and gentle. What I can't stand is the girls. I know he's horrible to them, always making them cry and everything, but he still has them to sleep with him and I hate that. I think he does it because he knows how much I loathe it. One night, he came into my room just after he'd had intercourse with a girl and made me fellate him. He smelt of her, was wet from her. I nearly vomited. I didn't want to do it, it was horrible, but he hit me until I did.

"Yes, he's made me perform analingus on him. I don't like it much, but I've got used to it. He's caned me, too. He's made me do just about everything to him. He took some photos once of me doing things to him. I don't know why. He photographed me fellating him, or him having me anally, or being whipped. That sort of thing. He's very demanding sexually, but I can cope with that. It's just the girls I can't stand. Sometimes I think he has them to hurt me, other times I think he's just mixed up and doesn't know what he wants."

On the subject of his flat-mate, Colin L is, as usual, quite assured.

"You've got to remember that he's a masochistic pansy. He likes proper men. I've never forced him to do anything he doesn't enjoy. I discovered he liked being whipped by accident and I just do it for him. It excites him and anything to do with sex excites me. I'm just exploring all possibilities and he likes doing things that other people might think disgusting. It's his nature. He's perverted, but you can't blame him for that. It's the way he gets his kicks, and he can leave the flat any time he likes. I never force him against his will. I admit some of our sex sessions are a bit way out, but it makes a change for me, and he likes it."

There is, obviously, a strong element of cruelty in Colin L's sexual relations with both men and women but significantly he is impotent, or rather partially impotent, only with women. Further investigations revealed that this was not, as was at first suspected, because his homosexual liaisons always included some form of semi-sadistic foreplay. He could, apparently, be perfectly potent with his flat-mate and other men without indulging in any form of cruelty. But with women he often, but by no means always, experienced difficulty in gaining and maintaining an erection. Yet, in all his sexual dealings, there was a disturbing element of sadism, of denigration of and revenge on the partner.

Colin L was enormously reluctant to talk about his early life. Whenever possible he preferred to describe his adolescent sexual adventures, many of which lacked any note of conviction, than to talk about his family, but slowly, by diligence and persistence, the facts were uncovered and pieced together they tell this story.

"My mother was a very powerful woman. A big woman, with a loud voice. She was kind, but roughly so. Any sign of affection sort of embarrassed her. My father, on the other hand, was completely opposite. He was small, timid and gentle. Physically, I resemble my mother. That's where I got my build, not from the old man. I think he must have been a masochist. I mean she wore the trousers in every other department, so why not in bed? Anyway, I think it was something like that. But in his quiet, docile way, Dad adored her. He never stood up to her, though, except over me. He always took my side. He was never afraid to show he loved me, and if I did anything wrong, he'd always protect me from my mother. I was very close to Dad and before I could begin to understand the position at all, I suppose I preferred him to Mum.

"I remember once she'd been on to me about something and she'd called me a 'sissy'. I was terribly upset. Dad had defended me as usual. He told her she shouldn't call me names like that, but she just went on and on. She sort of implied things about Dad that I knew were bad but didn't begin to understand. Anyway, she hit him eventually. She said we were both 'sissies' and hit him, cutting his eye. Afterwards, Dad sat with me and I said to him why was Mum like that, and I shall never forget what he said. He said I would understand some day that certain men needed women like that if they were going to be men at all.

"Now I think what he meant was that he was like me, bisexual, but that he was afraid of being queer. I think he must have been passive and attracted to men, but sort of hid it by playing a masochistic role with Mum. Of course, I didn't understand any of this at the time, and curiously, I didn't hate Mum, even then. I preferred Dad, but I suppose like all kids, I needed a mother and felt some special bond with her. I was scared of her, but I still loved her really.

"Then, when I was about fifteen she left us. Then I began to hate her. I had just discovered that I could ejaculate, and Mum caught me with one of my school friends up in my room after school. It was nothing serious. Just curiosity. He couldn't shoot off yet, and I was showing him. You know, just kid's stuff. We'd got our pants down, but we never even touched each other. Anyway, Mum discovered us and there was a terrible row when Dad came home. I stayed up in my room, as she told me to do. She didn't punish me in any other way. She just sent my friend home and told me to stay there. Anyway, there was a terrible to-do. I don't know what they said, but if my guess about Dad is right, I suppose she thought I was turning out like him and somehow blamed him. Anyway, next morning, she left. I've never seen her since. And I began to hate her, not really because she left me, in many ways it was better just being with Dad, but because it killed him. He changed. Oh, he put a brave face on it with me, but I knew he was miserable, desperately miserable, and if she'd stayed he'd never have got into the awful mess he did.

"Nothing seemed to interest him much, or so I thought. And then one night, I suppose I must have been about fifteen of sixteen, I woke up very late. He'd been drinking and somewhere he must have picked up a couple of toughs. Yes, youths. He made a pass at them, or I suppose he did, and they beat him up. He was a terrible mess, and of course it all came out. That was that. An interfering welfare worker decided it wasn't fitting for me to stay with him, so they sent me to a home. The old man died a few months later. I don't think he wanted to live any more. I stayed on in the home until I was old enough to look after myself. I learnt about homosexuals there all right. You couldn't avoid it. There was nothing else to do. No, I've never seen my mother since. I don't know whether she's dead or alive."

It is, of course, impossible to know if Colin L's assessment of his father's personality is accurate. It seems more likely that the man was a severely repressed homosexual who depended upon his strong-willed wife to keep him out of trouble. The woman's obvious edgy behaviour is more comprehensible if this picture be accurate. The son must have represented a dual threat, both a temptation to the father and a source of fear to the mother. In this explosive and unnatural situation, it is only logical that the child should respond to the most affectionate parent. The mother's ambivalence to him is perhaps explained by an exaggerated mistrust of all members of the male sex as a result of her experiences with her husband, and her own inability to show affection easily. By being brusque, she probably felt that she was encouraging her son "to be a man". In this light, her discovery of her son in masturbatory games with a school friend is likely to have seemed a token of her failure, the realisation of all her fears.

The root of Colin L's problem is, of course, his unresolved attitude to his parents. His natural affection and identification with his father is exaggerated both by his father's kindness and his mother's desertion. His natural impulse towards his mother was constantly frustrated, both by her manner and later by her absence. But he cannot wholeheartedly admire his father. Part of him revolts against the fragments of knowledge he has acquired about his father's true personality. He sees him as a masochist and fears that he is a homosexual. But these feelings are tempered and confused by his feelings of sympathy for his father's grief at being abandoned by his wife, and the awful predicament that resulted from this desertion. This, too, adds to his blame of his mother, whose defection he must fundamentally regard as his own rejection.

These unresolved antipathies and fears explain his cruelty. All sexual acts have become, for him, opportunities for revenge. Each girl he meets is a symbol of his mother. He feels a strong emotional impulse towards women, and it is natural for him to want to seek comfort and solace with them. He cannot do this, however, because he fears a repetition of his mother's rebuffs. Further, if he shows what to him seems like weakness, he fears that he will encourage the girl to take a dominant role and thus that the unhealthy pattern of his parents' own relationship will be repeated. This frustrated need for comfort and help quickly turns to cruelty and violence, both of which are increased by his periodic impotence. This functional impotence is also partly due to his fear of rejection by women and is harassed by his ambivalent attitude to his own sex. Thus he is revenging himself on his mother for past wrongs, and seeking to cover up his own present inadequacies.

Logically, we might therefore expect his homosexual liaisons to be more successful and, indeed, at times they are. From the evidence gleaned, it seems certain that

Colin L's homosexual impulse is marginally stronger than that towards the opposite sex. This is largely due to the fact that the male sex holds fewer fears for him because of his affectionate relationship with his father and his adolescent familiarity with homosexuality. But he cannot accept the idea of his own homosexuality. This, to him, implies total identification with his father and he attributes his father's "weakness" or "flaw" to his homosexuality. So he denigrates and abuses his homosexual partner. He is continually trying to prove that he is superior, that he is "above" homosexuality and only permits these attentions because they amuse him. He has to punish his partner because of his own self-loathing.

All this, of course, is hidden behind a brash exterior of extrovert bisexuality. His insistence on his bisexuality is a compromise which permits his homosexual indulgences but does not make him a true homosexual. So great is the fear and the self-loathing that he has taken complete refuge in an imaginary situation where he casts himself as a free-thinking, bisexual lothario, aggressive and expert, a superior being who demands adoration. Nowhere is this more clearly revealed than in his taking photographs of himself and his flat mate in homosexual practices. These photographs act as a visual confirmation of his superior role because in all the poses he is shown to be receiving "adoration", to be the object of sexual services, and also serve to remind the other man that he is a lesser creature, a slave to abused and used, in short, to be continually punished for his unequivocal homosexuality.

Colin L was recommended for intensive psychiatric treatment and only time can tell whether it is possible to help him resolve his frustrations and fears. His is a very exaggerated case, but the pattern of boastful bisexuality as a screen for unresolved ambivalent attitudes is a common one among male bisexuals. Partly this tendency is explained by the universal condemnation of male homosexuality which is often confused by an unsatisfactory relationship with the female sex.

The successful integrated male bisexual is not as uncommon as he may appear to be from the foregoing cases. He is, however, almost inevitably emotionally unfulfilled. Unlike his female counterpart, he is frequently a sensation seeker, the type of the Don Juan. His life is one long search for emotional fulfilment, but invariably a variety of sexual sensations is accepted as a substitute. He is an insatiable lover, seeking the maximum sexual pleasure from members of both sexes. In order to do this, he must accept his homosexual propensities, and this is invariably achieved. He is generally a genuine permissive, a man who believes that sexual activity should be enjoyed on as many levels and as completely as possible. Not uncommon in this group are the bisexual men who completely split their heterosexual and homosexual activities, who assume a virtually different persona for the two types of activity.

Tom N is such a man. To see him out with a girl is to see a picture of the clean-cut, professional young man. In a modishly cut dark suit, a discreetly colourful shirt and tie, with neat hair, he is the model young heterosexual male. He is gallant and courteous, easily paying those little attentions which women value so much. He is an active, accomplished lover with these girls, who describe him as tender and passionate. He prides himself on being a considerate lover, on his ability to share his pleasure with his female partner. But on other occasions, he dresses in a flamboyant manner. Too tight trousers, colourful sweaters often adorned with a chain belt and rather too much masculine jewellery. His hair is fluffed up and physically he seems to alter, to become more supple and girlish. On such occasions he frequents homosexual gathering places and takes the passive role in homosexual intercourse. Again he claims that he gets great pleasure from the activity and thoroughly enjoys being the passive recipient.

"I consider myself truly bisexual, that is, that I belong to both sexes. When I am with a girl, I am definitely male. I enjoy the sensation of being the stronger partner. The act of penetration is magnificently ego-building. It is total possession. The girl beneath me is mine. I have entered her and am there to take and give pleasure. I can't be a girl, I know that and I have no wish to dress as one, to be a transvestite, but I enjoy being a passive boy, wearing camp clothes and being penetrated. It is a totally different sensation. It makes me feel weak and vulnerable, whereas sleeping with a girl makes me feel strong and manly. There is no confusion between the two experiences, as far as I am concerned. They are quite separate. I have no wish to penetrate a man, none at all. I like to keep them separate. Both worlds are private, and I take great care that they should never become confused.

"No, I don't honestly think I could change, which means that I can't ever settle down. I suppose if I met a girl who meant everything to me, I could try, but I don't think I would succeed. Not completely. I could never choose to be exclusively homosexual. I am much more aware of playing a part in those situations, but I don't think I could do without them either."

Primarily masculine, Tom N nevertheless has a strong feminine impulse in him and he expresses this in terms of passive homosexuality. He handles his two worlds very successfully and there is no reason why he should not continue to do so, but there is no easy escape from this dual existence. As he grows older, this way of life is certain to be less satisfying, but the transfer to exclusive heterosexuality is likely to give rise to even more fundamental and difficult problems.

As one studies the bisexual male, it becomes increasingly obvious that the most important single factor which gives rise to problems and difficulties is the partially inherited, partly natural reaction to male homosexuality. Only a handful of bisexual men are able to accept their strong attraction to their own sex unequivocally. Even if, as is becoming increasingly possible, they are able to dismiss the moral implications of such a liaison, they invariably see homosexuality as a threat to their manhood. The male ego is an important but delicate mechanism. It thrives upon an essential approval and acceptance which any imputation of homosexuality can easily damage in the most alarming way. So often the problem degenerates into a war between the mind and the body. The body responds to its own sex, but the mind baulks at satisfying this response. Equally, the heterosexual response is often unfairly inhibited because of this ambivalent homosexuality and thus the initial fear is apparently confirmed while the problem itself is extended. Happily, the attitudes to male homosexuality are rapidly becoming more realistic, and it is therefore to be hoped that this powerful source of bisexual inhibition will gradually be removed. The bisexual already faces enough problems as a direct result of his nature without having to resolve the complex fears engendered by external attitudes to homosexuality.

CHAPTER 6: THE NYMPHOMANIAC

It must be stressed at once that all nymphomaniacs are not bisexuals, nor is there any necessary connection between the two types. It is, therefore, perfectly possible to write about nymphomania without touching upon the bisexual phenomenon. However, a proportion of nymphomaniacs are bisexual, if only insofar as their insatiable sexual desire causes them to have sexual relations with both men and women. However, some have a deeper connection than that and there is an extremely close link between their bisexuality and their nymphomania. In such cases it is often appropriate to regard the individual as either a bisexual or a nymphomaniac for clinical purposes. But for our purposes, no such division is necessary. Thus here and now we may talk of the bisexual nymphomaniac, although it should be clearly understood that nymphomania is here considered as an extreme and dramatic form of bisexuality. In other words, we regard the nymphomaniac as the logical and ultimate extreme of the bisexual phenomenon, at least as far as behaviour is concerned. It will quickly become clear, however, that the motives of the nymphomaniac are incredibly similar to those of the disturbed bisexual woman. So reliable and frequent is this similarity that it is undoubtedly true that many nymphomaniacs have been treated and regarded as the sole example of disturbed bisexual behaviour. Clinically the nymphomaniac is known to be disturbed. Her behaviour is immediately recognisable and, as we have said, is usefully regarded as a case apart from bisexuality. Commonly, therefore, at least as far as nomenclature is concerned, bisexuality is a term reserved for the non-disturbed, nymphomania for the very disturbed. Such categorisation is, obviously, false because it leaves out the many degrees of stressed behaviour between the integrated or successful bisexual and the genuine nymphomaniac.

Nymphomania is a term which has, perhaps regrettably, captured the public imagination with the result that it is frequently misapplied. Almost any willing or sexually voracious woman is referred to, either jokingly or derogatorily, as a nymphomaniac. However, this is a quite wrong use of the word, for such women are really no more than highly sexed. The true nymphomaniac is abnormally highly sexed. Sex dominates her life and causes it to be devoted to a search for an illusion of sexual fulfilment, often referred to as the perfect orgasm. She is sexually insatiable, unscrupulous and utterly selfish. For protracted periods, nothing else matters but her own sexual satisfaction, which is never obtained. The symptoms of nymphomania have often been likened to those of a skin disease. The victim is a prey to a constant exhausting itch which she is compelled, day by day, to try to assuage. But if nymphomania resembles a disease, it is a purely functional one. Without exception, nymphomania is itself the symptom of a psychological disturbance. The craving for sexual satisfaction may safely be regarded as a substitute for some other, more fundamental craving.

Nymphomania is not a common condition. Such women are always in a minority and, unfortunately, there is no reliable evidence to show how great or small is the incidence of bisexuality in nymphomania. This is a very difficult problem, for a woman whose life is virtually motivated by sexual need will obviously explore any avenue of possible fulfilment in her search. Because of this, we must not take evidence of her lesbian experiences as necessarily being evidence of bisexuality, any more than isolated instances would suggest that she is a true bestialist or compulsive masturbator. We can, however, discover women who are recognisably bisexual and recognisably suffering from nymphomania, and it is with just such a woman that our remarks here are concerned. What interests us is the already mentioned motive similarity between the nymphomaniac and the bisexual, albeit in an exaggerated form.

Because nymphomaniacs are, as a pure category of sexual behaviour, a very small minority, and because of the difficulty in establishing the true bisexuality of such women, our examples will be drawn from one woman who satisfies all doubts as to her bisexuality and her nymphomania. She is now a woman in her forties, but her earliest sexual experiences occurred well over twenty years ago. We can do no better than to relate her story, or part of it, and to draw our conclusions from her own evidence.

Carla M is the daughter of Italian parents, although she was born in Borneo. At the time, her father had an overseas post with a large engineering firm. The family were well off and Carla lacked for nothing. Virtually from her birth she was placed in the charge of a native nurse, and by the time she was five or six years old, apart from holidays in Italy, most of her time was spent with this woman. She remembers her parents at that time as being hazy, remote figures whom she saw at bedtime and on sporadic visits to the nursery. The central figure in her world was undoubtedly the nurse. Carla M is undecided about her exact age when her first sexual experience occurred, but she thinks she must have been six or seven years old. The nurse used to carry her into the native compound, a conglomeration of reed and wattle huts which clustered at the edge of the jungle some quarter of a mile from her parents' spacious bungalow. The nurse went to gossip with her friends, and the pretty, dark-haired little European girl was a source of great curiosity, as were her native counterparts to Carla. She distinctly remembers her surprise at the nudity of the native children and soon wanted to emulate them, although the nurse forbade this. She became distinctly aware of the anatomical difference between girls and boys. She soon began to compare her own genitals with those of the native girls, as well as with the mysterious protuberances of the little boys.

Soon she observed that both sexes openly fondled their genitals. Curiously the boys' little organs grew larger, and the girls seemed to derive satisfaction from their self-manipulation. Carla questioned her dark-skinned friends about this activity, and learned that it was "nice". She tried it herself but lack of expertise resulted in failure. Rather than admit this, she poured scorn on the habit, only to raise the ire of her native playmates, one of whom deftly showed Carla how it should be done. The practised brown fingers quickly produced the most delightful sensations in the little Italian girl and when she confessed this, her instructress informed her that it was even better if the area concerned was licked with the tongue. Thus Carla had her first experience of cunnilingus, a service she also performed on her friends. These activities which produced such startling but delightful sensations became a favourite pastime with the children. The native women, including the nurse, observed these practices but they merely laughed. True, the nurse remonstrated with Carla, but her own culture did not prohibit such customs among children and once she was convinced that her charge had no intention of revealing these secret games to her parents, she did not repeat her objections.

To Carla, the masturbation and cunnilingus was nothing more than a particularly pleasant game. She became a confirmed masturbator, seeking to experience as often as possible the quasi-orgasmic sensations which so delighted her. She would masturbate before going to sleep, before getting up in the morning and would undoubtedly enjoy some sexual game with the native children in the afternoon. Throughout this period, the genital attributes of boys continued to fascinate her, but apart from being an observer she had no direct genital contact with the boys. As is often the case in primitive customs, sexual play is permitted but the sexes are encouraged to play these games separately. Thus, apart from comparing genitals and observing each others' oral and masturbatory acts, the boys and girls had little to do with each other in this connection.

But at the age of ten, Carla returned to Italy with her parents. She was literally transplanted to a new environment and suffered many pangs at the loss of her nurse and even more at the sudden cessation of her games with the native children. Although she saw more of her parents they still seemed rather remote and the governess employed to educate and care for her was no substitute for the nurse in Borneo. Carla tried to introduce various little girls to her "native games" but with no success. Such things were regarded, by her correct European Catholic playmates, as dirty and sinful. Carla had to be content with masturbation, which became more and more frequent.

Her sexual discoveries increased, however, when she was thirteen. Carla was sent to spend the summer with an aunt and uncle in the country while her parents want on a cruise. Once again, Carla tried to interest others in her games. This time the object of her attentions was her cousin, a girl of eleven who indignantly refused to partake. However, Carla's attempt somehow reached the ears of the girl's brother, a boy of sixteen. Carla presumes that his little sister confided in him. He did not scorn and condemn Carla's interest in sexual matters. On the contrary, he sought her out and informed her that he knew what she had tried to do with his sister. He then boasted of the difference between boys and girls, but Carla assured him that her years of friendship with the children in Borneo had made her an expert on the subject. She described the attributes of the male sex, but the cousin was delighted to learn that she knew little about the male's erectile abilities and nothing at all about ejaculation. In return for a sight of her vagina, the boy proudly demonstrated his talents. The sight greatly aroused Carla who demonstrated female masturbation to him. She also told him about the sexual games played on the native compound, and he had little difficulty in persuading Carla to fellate him. In return he performed cunnilingus on her. Indeed they practised virtually all forms of sexuality except intercourse.

These adventures usually took place in the garden of the cousin's house and there, as Carla was soon to discover, their sexual frolics did not go unobserved. Her aunt's gardener, a man in his early thirties, soon began to take an interest in Carla, largely because he had observed her with her male cousin. Apart from showing her the various plants and explaining the rudiments of cultivation to her, he would slip his hand beneath her dress and play with her vulva. Carla delighted in this and had no objection to his removing her panties to perform other sexual acts upon her. The more she learned, the more she desired to experience. The gardener and her cousin made solitary masturbation almost unnecessary, and Carla happily noted that her sensations became increasingly pleasurable.

Amazingly, despite Carla's willingness to handle and mouth the gardener's organ, she left her aunt's house with her virginity intact. Presumably her age prevented the gardener taking this ultimate step. In the autumn she was sent to a strict Catholic boarding-school run by the sisters of a religious order. Despite the careful surveillance, Carla managed to have a number of lesbian relations there and she experimented as much as possible with the other girls. After the commencement of her menses, she claims that there was a marked increase in the strength of her orgasms, and that she became more and more interested in men. Her theoretical knowledge of intercourse now rapidly increased thanks to the superior sophistication of the older girls at the school. She believed, she said, that intercourse must be the most wonderful sensation in the world.

Carla was, however, sixteen before she first had intercourse with a man. By then she had filled out and her body, youthful and inviting, attracted a great deal of male attention. Carla knew this and played upon it. She wanted to lose her virginity but there was little opportunity. Carla flirted as openly as she dared with men, but only on rare occasions was she alone with them. But when she returned from school for the summer vacation in her sixteenth year, she found that her father had engaged a young chauffeur. A minor car accident had badly affected her father's driving confidence, hence this immediately attractive addition to the household staff. Carla developed an apparently passionate interest in motor-cars and spent as much time as she could in the garage where she flirted outrageously with the confused chauffeur. Eventually Carla realised that if she was to overcome the young man's reticence, she would have to take matters into her own hands. Thus one day she entered the garage and found the chauffeur lying on his back beneath the car. She squatted down, quickly unzipped his trousers and began to fondle him. The man's protestations, according to Carla, were vehement, but his aroused flesh soon overcame his common sense. Carla spread herself, skirts around her waist, on the back seat of the car. The amazed chauffeur threw himself upon her, and took her virginity.

"It hurt a little at first. It was like being entered by a piece of hot metal, but as he lay on me and the pain began to abate, I realised I was having an orgasm. I urged him on, thrusting my body up against him, and for the first time discovered what it was like, how wonderful, how indescribable it is to have a man inside one. I had an orgasm of such tremendous power, quite unlike anything I had ever known, and many more followed it. It was as though each movement he made, each plunging stroke produced an orgasm in me. My body became a receptacle for pleasure. Wave after wave of fire swept through me. I clung to him, drew him in to me. I never wanted it to stop. Never. And when he reached his climax, my brain seemed to explode and I was left weak and exhausted. Yet even then I tried to prevent him withdrawing. I wanted to go on and on. I think I realised, not in a complete, rational way, but instinctively then that no man was ever going to be able to satisfy me, and part of me hated him for abandoning me that way. His shrivelled, useless penis seemed a sort of offence. In a curious way, although it had been marvellous, I felt cheated."

This is a convenient point to pause and examine some of the finer points of Carla M's story, largely because we should understand that her voracious sexual explorations had all been a preparation for this first experience of sexual intercourse. It is for this that she had waited, and although the act of devirginisation is inevitably of paramount importance to all women, in Carla's case, simply because it was a conscious, longed-for goal, it becomes central to her subsequent sexual behaviour.

To return to the beginning, to her childhood in Borneo, we see at once that Carla did not enjoy the normal and proper relationship with her parents. She does not consciously blame them for her neglect, but her memories of them are as remote, well-dressed, glamorous figures perpetually *en route* for business of social functions. They were not familiar dependable creatures but strangers to whom she was tenuously related. Her natural need for emotional attachment was centred on her native nurse who, to all intents and purposes, replaced her parents. She it was who cared for her, played with her, answered her questions and Carla, with the amazing instinct of the child, soon came to see the nurse as an ally against her parents. This alliance was formed over the matter of sexual curiosity. It must be remembered that, shocking and reprehensible as Carla's games with the native children appear to us, they were, in context, quite natural, harmless and innocent. If there is any fault, the blame does not lie with the nurse or the children. Carla is merely the victim of a clash of alien cultures. The nurse knew enough to realise that her charge's participation in these games was contrary to the beliefs and practices of her European employers, but to her such an embargo on the accepted habits of her own people would seem arbitrary and silly. Her protestations to Carla were certainly more concerned with her fear of losing her job if the facts were known than any concern for Carla's moral welfare. That was not in question. The nurse herself and virtually all the people she knew would have grown up in an atmosphere of sexual freedom as exemplified by the childrens' games. She would see no harm in it, and once assured of Carla's silence would not interest herself particularly.

For Carla, however, the games took on a symbolic importance because of the nurse's hesitance about their suitability for her. This is not just a case of the increased attraction of the forbidden, but it is a tangible bond between the child and the one dependable person in her life. Instinctively Carla knew that there was something wrong with her relationship with her parents. She recalls once crying, not wanting her mother to leave her and being firmly reprimanded for "hysterical" behaviour. This tiny incident is not, however, unimportant. It fixes firmly a pattern of behaviour which Carla recalls quite clearly. Thereafter, even though still a young child, she felt inhibited in her parents' company, never daring to show the natural enthusiasms and affections of a little girl. This enforced reticence obviously made the lax easy-going nurse seem all the more preferable. With her Carla was fearless and uninhibited. Thus, once she understood that her parents would not approve of her sexual games, they became more attractive. They were a secret, something she shared only with the nurse. They represented her necessary private life, and they symbolically tied the nurse to her against her parents. By revealing the games, the nurse would be more threatened than Carla herself. Thus already, and quite accidentally, Carla had learned to use sex as a substitute for love and affection and as a means, albeit unrealistic, of binding people to her.

Thus the loss of the nurse when she returned to Italy became a genuine emotional blow. The one dependable permanent relationship she had been able to form was snatched from her. For a time she could not believe that the nurse would not suddenly appear in her Italian bedroom. Significantly, thereafter she seems to have formed no meaningful relationship other than in sexual terms. Her parents, although she now saw a little more of them, remained strangers to whom she presented a special face. Her governesses and tutors were unimportant shadows in her life. Her sexual knowledge and practices alone remained and because of her "rejection", *i.e.* the loss of the nurse, took on an even greater importance. When she discovered that her Italian contemporaries also did not want her sexual games, she interpreted this too as a rejection. She was, in short, a very lonely, very unhappy little girl. Her sole consolation was masturbation. The pleasurable sensations she could induce in herself were her only solace, a substitute for human contact.

Once we realise this, we see at once that her relationship with her male cousin and the gardener are quite logical. These are the two people who could enter her private world on her own terms, *i.e.* they shared her interest in sex, although their involvement, despite their behaviour, was undoubtedly less complex than Carla's. However, sex was the bond between them. Now, in Carla's mind, sex was love and affection, security and comfort. She was avidly interested in gaining as much information as possible and, largely because her knowledge of sex was natural, had grown without inhibitions, it was quite unconnected with fear and strangeness which would have made another child more reticent.

So far, Carla's lesbianism is also quite natural. Her games with the native girls and now her convent experiences were all occasioned by accidental necessity. She saw nothing wrong in her lesbian liaisons at boarding school because she had early learned to accept such practices as the norm. Because of her early life, heterosexuality was likely to seem more strange, more prohibited than lesbianism. At school, Carla identified with the rest of the girls. In such enclosed institutions lesbianism is generally a romantic involvement. The girls get great "crushes" on each other which pass quickly and often have only a minimal sexual expression. However, Carla's thirst for love was greater than her companions' and she suffered greatly. Her "crushes" were serious and her stormy school career was punctuated with despair as one "friend" after another abandoned her. Again she was forced to concentrate on sexual sensations. These never failed her. And so to the clinical sacrifice of her virginity. There was no suggestion of love in this. Carla's already overheated imagination made her reason that sexual intercourse would be the best, the most complete sexual sensation of them all, and in this she was not disappointed. However, her behaviour with the chauffeur is entirely selfish. She never once considered him. She took the initiative and all that interested her was her own physical sensations. To put it crudely, Carla now associated physical pleasure, *e.g.* orgasm, with love. These fleeting moments of physical delight are an end in themselves. They never fail her, whereas anyone she loves always does. In a sense she plays safe, concerning herself entirely with her own pleasure, which is dependable, and this is clearly revealed by her feelings of dissatisfaction after the incident and her sense of being cheated by the man.

Thereafter, Carla found it easy to find men willing to satisfy her. She was both ruthless and selfish, reasoning that her partners were sufficiently rewarded by having a willing young girl to render any other concern immaterial. Her opportunities, however, were severely limited, but she became cunning and inventive. She offered herself, quite unequivocally and unabashed, to any man with whom she happened to be alone.

"It was like a raging fire in me," she said. "Only a penis, hot and hard, could bring me relief and so I did it with whoever I could, wherever I could."

She was, of course, still at school and still her lesbian activities continued. Since they became more and more aggressive, she was inevitably discovered and expelled in shame. Her shocked and uncomprehending parents provided Carla with a series of male tutors, convinced that her expulsion proved her exclusive interest in her own sex. Carla succeeded in seducing three of these men and this halcyon period ended abruptly when Carla was discovered to be some months pregnant.

"My parents were really terribly unimaginative," she said. "I was packed off to the country, to my aunt, and I had the baby there. It was adopted at birth. Unfortunately, the gardener had gone, and his replacement was too old for my taste. However, I renewed my relationship with my cousin who sometimes took me two or three times a day. But he was only there at weekends. After the baby was born, I used to go for long walks and often found a man in a field or working on some remote farm who would satisfy me. It was all I thought about. And always it was the same. I would have two or three orgasms but they were never enough. I always hated the men unless they could grow hard again quickly. My cousin was the best. That was why I conceived the idea of having two men, one after the other. I persuaded my cousin to bring a friend down for the weekend, a friend who would be willing to have me. There was no shortage of such men. And he agreed. He had me first and, as I said, it was always good with him, and as soon as he had finished, the other man entered me. I thought that now I would find the last, big orgasm which always seemed to elude me, but it wasn't like that. The boy did his best but I just went on having orgasm after orgasm until he, too, was exhausted. The big one never came."

And so the goal of the search was defined. The big orgasm, the perfect body-shattering, mind-assuaging sensation that will leave her fulfilled and exhausted. Since Carla experiences frequent and good orgasms, since, physically, she has none of the problems that dog many women, it may seem, at first strange that such a goal should be so important and so elusive. The perfect orgasm, however, in most cases of nymphomania stands for the permanent, satisfying love relationship. The nymphomaniac seeks the great orgasm as other women seek the right partner. The connection, of course, is not so clear-cut as that. The woman does not make this connection consciously, but she frequently believes that the partner who could give her such an orgasm would be a person she could love.

Indeed, it was precisely for this reason that Carla married. She met a young English soldier serving in Italy and found him to be as sexually inexhaustible as herself. Or nearly so. With him she believed that she would find the great experience and when he asked her to marry him she readily agreed. Normally her parents would have opposed the match, but in the light of Carla's past they were pleased to see her, as they thought, settled. Carla sees their enthusiasm for her marriage as another rejection. As far as she is concerned, they simply wanted to be rid of her.

"So we were married," Carla said, "and at first everything was fine. He was still in the army and we had sex every moment we could. I was happy. He never failed me and if I didn't quite reach the big one, I certainly came close to it. He was as crazy about sex as me. Sometimes he would bring a group of his friends home and he never minded if they had me. Sometimes I would have three or four men in one night. That could exhaust me physically, but never really satisfy me. And then he was posted back to England. I went with him and again everything was fine. But he changed. He no longer brought his friends home and when he was discharged from the army, he wasn't enough for me any more. He would be away all day, and I would have this longing. Soon I began to go with other men. The milkman, the repair men. Anyone. Once there was a gang of men doing something to the pipes in the street opposite my house. I had them all. One by one they would come in. I would stand at the window naked, inviting them. Of course, the neighbours talked and my husband found out. He made it quite clear to me. The way we had lived in Italy was one thing, but here, in his country, I had to be a proper wife. I tried. I truly tried to heed his warnings, but I couldn't help myself. There were other men, even a young boy who delivered the groceries. It was hopeless. He divorced me and I could not defend the way I had behaved."

Carla drifted from man to man. She was virtually a prostitute, but then she found a job and began to have lesbian relationships again. She was, as always, lonely, and this loneliness was dramatised by her being in a strange country. She drifted into pubs and clubs, including those frequented by lesbians. She thought, at this time, that perhaps her search had failed because of the men she had known. She began to have lesbian affairs again in the hope of achieving her goal. She met a man who arranged "private parties", or organised orgies in which Carla became an eager participant. In group sex, indulging herself with men and women, often at the same time, she hoped to find what she was looking for. Again these athletic sessions exhauted her physically but left her otherwise unsatisfied. She reached the lowest point of degradation.

"I remember at one party, a man had me anally at the same time as another did it the usual way. This was good for me, but when they had finished I joined another woman. And so it went on, for hours. I passed out with a man on top of me, and when I regained consciousness, there was another man in his place."

Hysterical, weeping Carla had the first of a long series of nervous breakdowns. In hospital, as soon as she was sufficiently recovered, she began to have lesbian and heterosexual relations with her fellow patients. She became an embarrassment to the staff and was discharged. Since that time, Carla has lived for sex. She has been a prostitute at times, but mostly she drifts from one man or woman to another, seldom working but relying on others to keep her in return for her body. This sad, exhausting existence is punctuated periodically by nervous breakdowns. Her search goes on. She has tried flagellation. Her body bears the scars left by sadists, evidence of the time when she thought the secret of the unattainable orgasm might lay in the endurance of pain. She expects to be abandoned. She knows that even if someone cares enough about her, she will soon tire of them sexually and will seek new partners. There have been several abortive suicide attempts. Carla is no longer beautiful. She looks older than her years, tired, edgy and exhausted.

This then is the terrifying plight of the sex-driven woman, the nymphomaniac. There is little real help that can be given to a woman in Carla's predicament. She has no conception of love save as something she has been denied. Simple sexual pleasure no longer holds much attraction for her. Her exhausted body is now only concerned with the unattainable, that man or woman who, by some unknown superhuman trick, will ease the painful longing in her body. Under other circumstances, she would be an emotional neurotic, but as it is the whole impulse of her life has become inextricably involved with sex. Happiness, peace, fulfilment all depend upon the perfect orgasm which will leave her body peaceful, her mind comforted and give her a mysterious assurance that she is loved. But the flaw lies in the fact that each new experience can be bettered. Over the years, Carla M has abandoned everything to concentrate upon this quest. She has lost her self-respect and almost her reason. She is sexually dominated and eternally frustrated.

Thus from this account it should be obvious that the nymphomaniac is not the ideal partner people like to imagine. She is not a glamorous creature, but a sad piece of human wreckage. Denied and frustrated, she is condemned to loneliness which no degree of physical intimacy can possibly expel. She is bisexual because any avenue is worthy of exploration in her fruitless search. To Carla it truly makes no difference whether she gives herself to a man or a woman. She is the supreme bisexual because the sex, the looks, the personality of her partner are totally unimportant. She long ago ceased to have any human concern for them. In a sense, she does not even notice them. They are merely ciphers who might be able to supply what she needs. Since they are doomed to failure, she discards them unremorsefully. Those who seem to promise to succeed are inevitably destroyed by her inhuman insatiability. This factor, of course, this lack of care for her lovers of either sex, only increases her loneliness. She is an outcast, reduced to a body that must be endlessly and pointlessly pleasured. For these reasons, it is no exaggeration to say that the nymphomaniac is not only the most extreme manifestation of the bisexual personality, but also the saddest figure in the whole of sexual pathology.

CHAPTER 7: THE SATYR

In Greek Mythology, the Satyr was the name given to the woodland deities when they assumed semi-human form. According to the ancient stories, these forest gods turned themselves into a curious mixture of human and animal beings. At their most human they possessed the bodies of men but adorned with cloven feet, tails and animals' ears. At other times, the head and torso of a man was joined to the hindquarters of a horse or goat. This amalgam of the human and the animal kingdoms is symbolic of two attributes — the godliness of the deity and his lust. No man could achieve such a mutation, and these deities were believed to be sexually voracious. Human beings have always regarded their superiority over the animal kingdom as being symbolised by their questionable ability to control their sexual desires, and "animality" has, over the years, become a virtual euphemism for sexual lust and, on occasions, prowess. Artists have, therefore, frequently made capital of the fact that the satyrs of mythology were frequently endowed with the large sexual parts of animals, *e.g.* the horse, and were thus regarded as being more insatiable than mere humans. Further, because men and women have constantly confused genital organ size with ability, the satyrs were held to be exceptionally good lovers. Thus men feared that this sexual superiority, at bottom traceable entirely to the largeness of the satyrs' organs, would draw their women to them and, indeed, no mythological female appears to have been dissatisfied by her human/animal lover.

In adopting the word "satyr" and its derivation "satyriasis" to describe the male's abnormal thirst for sexual intercourse, we recognise traces of that disapproval of the male urge which we have already discussed. The strength of the masculine sexual impulse is taken for granted and, as we have already pointed out is, to a certain degree, tolerated. But once that degree is exceeded, the hypersexual male is simply, even in supposedly unemotive clinical terms, equated with the animals. However, it is a respectable and accurate terminology, and, in this work at least, we can ignore the element of judgement in the term. Similarly, the element of envy which is also sometimes ignorantly attached to the satyr, who is regarded merely as a sexual adventurer with some special "knack" for obtaining intercourse. Satyriasis, then, is the extreme need for sexual activity on an abnormal scale. Or, to put it more simply, it is the masculine equivalent of nymphomania.

It is important to state, however, that the conditions of nymphomania and satyriasis have, generally speaking, only superficial similarities. Certainly both are represented by a feverish and abnormally frequent desire for sexual relations, and victims of both conditions are invariably sexually dominated. But, as we saw with regard to nymphomania, these are only symptoms of the basic problems which create, in their turn, further complications. We cannot, however, carry the comparison much further with any reliable degree of accuracy. We have already discussed the fundamental difference in sexual approach and attitudes between men and women, and this factor is very influential in differentiating between nymphomaniacs and satyrs. Further, we must realise at once that the very basic differences in quality, frequency and attainability of the male and the female orgasm play a significant part here. If he is not functionally impotent, the male can easily achieve a satisfactory orgasm. It need be little more than simple ejaculation, an almost automatic process which can be brought about quickly and which is the essential, logical end of all masculine sexual arousal. The male does not have to strive for orgasm, he is virtually assured of it. It is a much more physical phenomenon than female orgasm, by which we mean that it is only slightly affected by psychological and external factors. And, of course, it is impossible for a man to have any satisfactory sexual relationship without achieving orgasm, while this is not necessarily true of women. The result of all this is a reduction in importance and meaning of the male orgasm and we cannot, therefore, expect the satyr's behaviour to be motivated, as the nymphomaniac's invariably is, by a search for the perfect orgasm. To a man, any orgasm is good enough, and the perfect one, if such a phenomenon can be said to exist, is relatively easily achieved.

There are, of course, satyrs who parallel the case of Carla M discussed in the last chapter in so far as their satyriasis is a symbolic search for love and affection, but such men are very few and far between. The male does not connect love and sex so closely and so automatically as a woman. Of course, the average man sees sexual intercourse as the logical expression of his love for his partner, but he can also regard sexual activity as a purely physical sensation with no emotional connotations. This is very often the rationalisation of a married man's philandering and it is not without genuine psychological truth. But this ability to divorce sexual indulgence from emotional involvement means that all men, and satyrs in particular, are seldom, in their sexual behaviour, seeking love and stable affection.

It would rather be true to say that satyriasis is more often a case of ego assertion. The male expresses himself naturally in sexual terms. His unique erectile phallus is a very symbol of his masculinity. Physically and symbolically it resembles a weapon and in its exaggerated employment, the satyr is frequently concerned to confirm not only his manhood, but also his identity. By penetrating as many women as possible, he feels that he is impressing himself upon them, that he is gaining, in a sense, a sort of perpetuity. No man can readily believe that his literal invasion of a female body can leave it unchanged, and thus the satyr is merely confirming his existence, affirming himself as a member of the male sex. The importance of this point is more readily grasped if we understand that belonging to the male sex is of vital concern to a male person whereas woman tend to think of themselves always in isolated terms, as individuals. His reasons for needing to do this are those which always result in some identity problem, *e.g.* lack of parental love, sibling rivalry, role confusion etc., etc. And this motivation is common among men and, consequently, the male satyr is more frequently found than the female nymphomaniac. He is, like all excessives, unsure of himself, and his exaggerated sexuality should be understood as an attempt to fix and grasp his own persona in the general context of a masculine brotherhood.

However, it must also be admitted that the ego-affirming satyr is very seldom bisexual. Like the nymphomaniac, it is extremely difficult to ascertain the true connection between and incidence of bisexuality in satyriasis, but we can certainly affirm that there is far less blurring between the bisexual and the heterosexual satyr than there is in similar categories of nymphomania. This is largely due to the fact that, as we have indicated, there is a much stronger social and moral aversion to male homosexuality than there is to lesbianism. This, obviously, restricts the satyr's indulgence in homosexual practices, but far more importantly we should understand that the ego-affirming satyr is not interested in impressing his own sex. It is women who can, by their very nature, affirm his identity. Thus, this type of satyr is seldom bisexual save by force of circumstances. Simply because the need for sexual release does not cease the moment the satyr is removed from female company, he will, in such all-male societies as the armed services, or prison, readily take to homosexual practices, but it is very seldom indeed that these are regarded as anything other than an essential substitute.

Nevertheless, bisexuality does play an important part in another major group of satyrs. However, we must not look, as we have become accustomed to do, for overt signs of homosexuality, for the bisexual satyr is almost exclusively heterosexual, at least in his interpretation of the facts. Satyriasis, regarded as the extreme of bisexuality, is always and invariably the result of a very dramatic failure on the part of the individual to accept his dual sexual nature. In psychological terms this results in an exaggerated case of substitution and over-compensation, with all the attendant tensions and complications that this inevitably entails. All this, and more, will be illustrated by the case of Paul V, a young man of twenty-six who came to medical attention as a result of nervous debility and marked tension.

Paul V is good-looking, intelligent and charming. Physically he is in good health. However, he seems now subdued. Few subjects interest him, surprisingly not even himself, except for his sex life. About this he is enthusiastic and voluble. Since his sixteenth year, his history has been one of gradually accelerating decline. Up until the age of sixteen, he was a conscientious grammar school pupil with a decided leaning towards the arts. His progress, marks and school reports were good. But from then until he left school at eighteen, he sank lower and lower in the form. His G.C.E. "A" level results were disappointing and his parents and teachers had to abandon their plans for him to continue to university. Things improved for a time after leaving school. He did casual work and seemed happy. But the need to obtain some sort of permanent job with prospects was impressed upon him and thus began a series of office jobs, all of which ended in disaster. He lost his first three jobs because of a marked lack of attention. Thereafter he was sacked for continual absence and lateness. When challenged by his parents about this, he always claimed that he was bored, or over-worked, or victimised. Soon he lost a job after being caught *in flagrante delicto* with a young female member of the staff. This had happened on two subsequent occasions. For a time there was an improvement. Paul V left home and managed to hold down a reasonably good job, but eventually complaints were made against him by his female colleagues and Paul was again dismissed. After this he again began to drift from job to job, always being sacked throught inefficiency, lateness, or absence. It became increasingly difficult for him to obtain employment, and his last job was as an assistant in a small, privately-owned bookshop. The owner arrived at the shop at eleven o'clock one morning to find the "closed" sign on the door. Letting himself in, he surprised Paul V in the back office copulating with a girl on the desk. His mild nervous breakdown followed this incident, and after a short stay in a mental home, he was discharged because of a sudden renewal of his sexual exploits, but he was referred, by his distressed but kindly parents, for private analysis. Over a period of weeks, the following statement was obtained from the patient about his work and his sexual appetite.

"I could never keep a job because I could never concentrate. I know now that I was avoiding the truth when I said I was bored. None of the jobs I had were particularly boring, and in any case I didn't stay in a lot of them long enough to find out. As for being over-worked, well, that was just a lie. I could have coped easily, if only I'd have put my mind to it. But that's the problem, you see, I just can't get down to work. I can't concentrate. Every day, ever since I left school, I have been thinking about sex, about women.

"You see, I'd have the best intentions in the world. I

knew what a hopeless mess I was getting into and I would determine to do something about it. But then, the moment I woke up I'd have a terrible erection. Not the sort that goes away after you've peed either. No, I'd have an erection all the way to work, and just looking at the girls in the bus or on the train would make me more and more excited. And so when I got to work, all I could think about was having sex. I'd look at all the girls and think what I could do with them. I couldn't wait for lunchtime when I'd hope to find a girl. And so the morning would pass without my having done anything. In the lunch hour I'd chat up any girl I could find. I used to go to a club where they played records for dancing. Sometimes I'd meet a girl there, but it wasn't often I could do anything about it then. The only thing that helped was if I got a prostitute in my lunch hour. I did that as often as I could, but I couldn't afford it as often as I liked. Sometimes I could have a girl in the lunch hour without paying, but it wasn't easy. But if I could have sex then I could work in the afternoons for a couple of hours or so. And then it would start all over again.

"In the evenings I used to rush home and then go out with some girl, or if I hadn't got a date go prowling around looking for one. I began to take jobs that made getting sex easier. For example, I worked in a couple of offices where I was left in charge for an hour or so while the rest of the employees went out. Then I'd have a girl friend up and do it in the office. Or I'd take a job that took me out into the town on messages, or to another building. I always lost these because I took so long either because I was chasing some girl or was with a prostitute.

"The first time I got caught was at a big company I was working for. They had these big open plan offices and I used to sit there for hours surrounded by girls. I pretended to work but really I was listening to the sound of their nylons as they crossed their legs, looking at the way their breasts strained against their clothes, trying to see up their mini-skirts. I'd have an erection for three or four hours at a time, and the morning would just pass in a sexual haze.

"Anyway, there was one girl there and I knew she was easy. I used to date several of the girls but didn't get very far with them. However, one of the messenger boys told me one day in the loo that she'd let him feel up her dress, so after that I never took my eyes off her. I was absolutely obsessed by her. Anyway, one morning she had to go down to the legal filing room. The legal documents were kept in a separate place from the central files, and there was no permanent staff in there. So I followed her down and began chatting her up. She responded, so I kissed her, but she wasn't very keen because she didn't feel safe there. But I grabbed her and kept on talking and touching her breasts and she began to give way. I got my hand up her skirt and after a bit of a struggle, inside her pants. She was all wet and ready. Nothing could have stopped either of us then. I whipped her panties off and got my penis out. I had her up against a filing cabinet. It was great, I can tell you. Sliding up into her. I was so excited, all that wet warmth tugging at me, that it only took a minute or so, but just as I was beginning to come, the head of the legal department walked in. You should have seen his face! I bet he would have liked to change places with me. Anyway, he just stood there while we finished, and then he marched me off to the boss, after I'd fastened my trousers, and I was out on my ear.

"After that though, despite being sacked, I felt more confident about approaching girls at work. I had a lot of success after that. Things should have got better then, but somehow they didn't. The fact that I knew I could have a girl more or less whenever I wanted was just as distracting as not having one at all. I just used to sit and wonder when I could next create an opportunity, when she'd let me. That sort of thing. And then, of course, because I had quite a lot of success, I got even bolder. I just tried it on with anyone who took my fancy, and that led to complaints being made against me. I got scared, however, when I saw that with my record I was virtually unemployable. That's why I determined to really make a go of the bookshop. It was a matter of pride. I wanted to prove myself, and there were no permanent female distractions there. I suppose that's why I cracked up when I was found out again. Because of the pride, I mean. I used to take girls there, but not so often and only in the lunch hour. But that morning, a girl I'd met at a party just dropped by and I couldn't resist. So I locked up the shop and took her into the back office. If I hadn't been a fool and taken my trousers and briefs completely off, I might have got away with it. But when I heard the boss coming, there wasn't time to get my things on, so I just carried on. And so I got caught again."

What Paul V describes are the classics symptoms of satyriasis, an overweening, insatiable interest in sex which dominates all other considerations. There was, as he admits, nothing intrinsically wrong with his jobs but he was quite unable to concentrate on or really care about them. His mind was continually occupied with sexual fantasies and schemes to have intercourse at the earliest possible opportunity. However, his account, clear and accurate as it is, gives no clue as to his reasons for wishing to have intercourse so often. When questioned Paul V could offer no further explanation. He described his sensations during the act enthusiastically and with a somewhat boastful air, but he spoke in purely physical terms. It was obvious that he enjoyed the pursuit and seduction of women, but his enjoyment of this and of intercourse was not exceptional. He experienced no sexual problems and seemed perfectly happy in recalling the many incidents which had helped to destroy his working life. The only explanation he could offer was that he was abnormally highly-sexed and simply had to have intercourse more often than most men.

Having found no real evidence in these statements and discussions of a disturbed motive for Paul's exorbitant sexuality, his analyst fastened upon the two statements which seemed slightly out of key to the rest of his narrative. The two statements in question are those which concern his being discovered in sexual intercourse by his employers. In both instances, Paul's voice betrayed unusual excitement in the recollection of the incidents. Further, his remark that the first man observed him completing the act and the fact that Paul boastfully felt the man would have liked to change places with him suggested a possibly worthwhile avenue of exploration. This impression was confirmed by his detailed explanation of the fact that he had undressed in the bookshop, that had he merely unfastened his trousers he could have avoided discovery. Even more important is the fact that he made a conscious decision not to attempt to hide what he was doing when he heard his employer approaching.

Normally, these details, so clearly remembered by Paul, and related with obvious excitement, would be forgotten or suppressed. It is the act which usually obsesses the patient, not the circumstances of its discovery. And at no time does Paul evince any shame or embarrassment when he recollects these incidents. Even the most hypersexed satyr is usually discomfited if he is interrupted in the midst of sexual intercourse, and certainly does not take such pains to relate the details. Working backwards from this information, it is also possible to see that Paul deliberately chose to exercise his sexual potential in circumstances which greatly increased his chances of being discovered or observed. Of course, it is possible, as Paul himself claimed, that given the circumstances of his satyriasis, he had no choice, that considerations of time and place were completely overidden by his persistent desire. However, Paul's doctor was not satisfied by this explanation and asked Paul to describe as fully as possible his reactions on being discovered.

"Well, I don't know. Interested, I suppose. I mean I was interested in the incredulous expression on their faces. I liked the feeling that I was being envied. I knew they didn't really blame me, that they would have done the same in my place. And, I suppose, I mean this sounds awful, but I felt a sort of pride. You see, I'm pretty big down there, I have a big penis, and when I drew it out, on both occasions, I could see they were surprised. That made me feel good."

There is, we note at once, no feeling of concern for his job, no feeling of shame or embarrassment, but a very lively curiosity and careful observation of the intruder's reactions. These remarks confirmed the doctor's previous suspicions. He had concluded, from the details given in Paul V's first narrative, that they were indicative either of exhibitionism or, more specifically, of a wish to be observed by men in an explicitly masculine sexual situation. Almost any other man, satyr or not, and particularly one who is so remarkably free from normal confusion under extraordinary circumstances, would seek to cover his body, to instinctively hide his genitals from the intruder. In answer to further questions, Paul confirmed that this was exactly the reaction of the girls who turned away and quickly lowered their skirts. Thus we may interpret Paul's reactions as a deliberate display of his genitals to the men who interrupted him. This could still be evidence of simple exhibitionism except that it is a characteristic of the exhibitionistic male that he seeks only to display himself to women. The confirmed exhibitionist is invariably shocked into confusion when observed by a member of his own sex, and seeks to hide at once what he otherwise proudly displays. Unless, of course, he is homosexual. The doctor then proceeded to question Paul about homosexuality. The young man calmly affirmed that he had no homosexual experiences at all and evinced all the usual heterosexual reactions to the subject, except that he was quite calm about it and affected a rather lofty disinterest in the subject. The true heterosexual reaction is usually more strongly worded than Paul's and occasions more obvious emotion.

Still in search of proof of his rapidly growing theory, the doctor questioned him about group sex and his participation therein. At once a stream of confessions were offered. While still at school Paul had observed two of his friends making love to a girl. He and a male friend had shared the same prostitute on two occasions. At this point, Paul waxed eloquent about "watching his big phallus slide in and out of her, the way his bottom clenched and relaxed as he moved in her and then went very tight when he came." He admitted that he liked the sensation of being observed in his turn by his friends, ostensibly because it excited them anew and thus prolonged the sexual activity, a desire he invariably experienced in any sexual situation. Further, when Paul left home he frequently shared girls with various men friends, encouraged male acquaintances to have intercourse with their girl friends in his flat, on which occasions he invariably shared the same bed with his own girl and was thus able to watch.

This exhaustive, highly-detailed, excitingly described recollection of incidents confirmed the analyst's suspicions that Paul V was, in fact, a repressed or latent homosexual and that this repression or lack of self-knowledge, whichever it may be, was fundamentally responsible for his satyriasis. However, he could gain no further information. To repeated questioning, Paul V maintained that he had no homosexual experience and calmly insisted that his very condition removed any fear he may have had of homosexuality. It was simply a matter of indifference to him. Consequently, the doctor left the subject and concentrated on Paul's early life and his relationship with his parents, a line of investigation which quickly proved to be very fruitful.

Paul V has only the faintest recollection of his father, for he died when the boy was three. His actual knowledge of his father has been learned from his mother. Fortunately, he was too young for the loss to have any real or permanent effect upon him and he claims that the years alone with his mother were uncomplicated and happy. Naturally, Paul was very close to his mother. She was, however, still a young and attractive woman. Six years later she remarried. This new, potentially traumatic, situation also appears to have left young Paul unscathed. He was given time to grow accustomed to the idea and found that he responded to his stepfather's overtures. He had been presented to Paul as someone who was going to love and take care of them both, and the man's behaviour bore out this promise. Paul suddenly found himself entering a new, masculine world. His stepfather played with him, took him out and generally created a new dimension to his life. Paul was, in fact, pleased by the marriage and it is significant that when recalling this part of his life he refers again and again to his stepfather's good looks. The man was still young and this plus his handsomeness greatly impressed Paul. He seemed a more attractive, lively father than those of his friends. However, Paul insisted that he hated this man and that life had subsequently become unbearable with him. This statement seemed at variance firstly with Paul's acceptance of the marriage and with his present relationship with the stepfather who had been compassionate and helpful to Paul throughout his illness and his analysis. The root of this claimed hatred apparently stemmed from Paul's accidental witnessing of his mother and stepfather making love.

"I don't know, I suppose I was ten or eleven. I had woken up and was going to the bathroom. Their door was open, their bedroom door, and the light was on. My stepfather was lying on top of my mother and at first I was frightened. I thought he was hurting her. But then I saw her face. Her head was thrown back and she looked ecstatic. The moment I saw her expression I knew she liked whatever it was he was doing. As I watched, I could see her breasts and all his body moving on her. I had never seen a naked male adult before, and it fascinated me. But I was afraid of being caught, so I crept back to bed and just lay there wondering about what I had seen."

Under great stress, Paul V continued:

"I couldn't forget about it. My stepfather always used to tuck me up at night, and a few days after that, I asked him to lay on top of me. It didn't mean anything. I had no idea what it meant at all. It was just that what I had seen him doing had obviously made my mother so happy and I didn't see why he couldn't do it to me. She said he was going to love and take care of us both, and I didn't see why he shouldn't lie naked on top of me, like he had with her. It didn't mean anything. Just child's foolishness. He just laughed and told me to go to sleep."

At this point in Paul V's story the doctor's suspicions are both confirmed and particularised. At a very early age, Paul V felt a natural but definite homosexual attraction to his stepfather whose naked body regularly featured in his dreams and fantasies. Although it is true that the child did not understand the true implications of what he saw or asked, he felt, for the first time, excluded. Quite simply, it seemed to him that his mother was receiving more favours than he, more of the love and affection he had begun to take for granted from his stepfather. Normally under such circumstances, we would expect Paul to be jealous of his mother, but he does not appear to have been. His energies were rather concentrated on his stepfather whose attention he continually sought to secure. However, this fact is covered by an insistence upon his hatred of his stepfather which is a naive example of compensation. Feeling himself neglected, Paul in fact took refuge in an unconvincing myth of petulant dislike.

At this point in the investigations, Paul became very uncooperative and further information was only obtained by the use of so-called "truth drugs" which effectively removed his inhibitions and enabled him to fill in the gaps in his story.

At the age of thirteen, Paul observed his stepfather masturbating. His mother was pregnant and during her confinement Paul and his stepfather were alone in the house together. Paul tried, unsuccessfully, to persuade the man to let him share his bed. In desperation he went to the parental bedroom late at night, intending to feign illness or unhappiness at his mother's absence, in order to sleep with his stepfather.

"The bedside lamp was on and he was sprawled across the bed. He was nude except for his socks and his underpants which were around his knees. His penis was enormous and he was caressing it. I got an erection watching him. I thought he was beautiful. I wanted to go in, but I didn't dare. I waited until he finished, watched him collapse on the bed exhausted, and then I went back to my own room and masturbated."

The next night, when Paul went to bed, he waited anxiously for his stepfather to come to bid him goodnight. When he did, Paul threw off the bedclothes to reveal his nude body and masturbated. He received a lecture from his stepfather, a mild rebuke in retaliation to which Paul informed the man that he had observed him masturbating. The stepfather slapped him and thereafter Paul became openly hostile. He still sought opportunities to observe his stepfather but no longer entertained any more specific hopes. Soon he could ejaculate and learned more about masturbation from his peers, although he did not indulge in mutual play with these boys.

The climax to this long unresolved flirtation with homosexuality came in his sixteenth year which, it will be remembered, was also the start of his decline. The agent of this trauma was Paul's uncle, the younger brother of his stepfather who, for a short period, stayed with the family and, because of the lack of room, shared a bedroom with Paul.

"He was even better looking than my stepfather, and younger. He'd been abroad and was deeply tanned. He was just staying with us until he got a job and was used to being in England again. I used to lie awake watching him preparing for bed. I used to get an erection just looking at him nude or semi-nude. One night I asked him to tell me about how babies were born, though I knew perfectly well. He was undressing at the time and I kept pretending not to understand, asking for more details. I asked him what it was like to have intercourse, and as he told me he began to get excited. I showed him my erection, and we talked about masturbation. He was surprised to see how big I was. It was easy after that. I led him on and on. He was frustrated, he needed sex badly. We did everything together, every night. It was the happiest time of my life."

When the uncle left, it was a severe blow to Paul but he had, temporarily, resigned himself to his homosexuality. He was more confident and quickly formed a fairly intense relationship with an older boy at school. Soon Paul made homosexual advances which the boy rejected. Instead he told Paul that masturbation led to homosexuality, that it was wrong and disgusting. Paul valued his friend's good opinion and his words had a genuine effect. He resolved not to masturbate. He sublimated his strong homosexual urges and, under the guidance of the older boy, had his first heterosexual experience. This made him completely acceptable to his friend and heterosexual intercourse became a substitute for his homosexual practices.

Whenever he was attracted to a member of his own sex, as he was, increasingly, he sought out a willing girl and reaffirmed himself as a heterosexual, and therefore acceptable, person.

Now a new and final dimension was added to his work failures. In each job he took he found himself deeply attracted to some young male colleague. Because of his fear, he transferred this attraction to his female colleagues. His lack of concentration was in fact due not to the irresistability of surrounding female charms but in his conscious observation of them as a "protection" against his "unnatural" leanings. He felt compelled to prove his normalcy by copulating as often as possible with girls because of his intense erotic attraction to men. He confessed that during intercourse he always fantasised about some male acquaintance or some young man he had observed. One incident, related in detail, will suffice to complete the picture.

"At the place where I was sacked for doing it with the girl in the filing room, there was this messenger boy. He was about seventeen and very attractive. I couldn't bear it when he came to my desk, and he was very friendly and used to talk to me a lot. We used to talk about sex, about the girls. Once, completely by accident, I went to the lavatory and he was in there. I knew I shouldn't, but I stood next to him and started talking about girls. He told me about this girl who was easy, the one I eventually had. I was watching him and I could see that he got excited so I kept on asking him about what he'd done with the girl. And then he had an erection and I just put my hand on it. He grinned and said, 'You like that, too, do you?' I didn't say anything. I put my other hand on his bottom. He liked it. He told me there was a boy in the packing department who liked to play around with men too. He said it was safer down there. So he zipped up and I went back to my office. But knowing he was down there, I couldn't stay away. So I went down to the packing department and into a toilet they had there. He was there and so was the boy he'd told me about. This boy, this other one, he was in one of the cubicles with the door open and he had his trousers and briefs down. I knew I shouldn't, but I had to. I did things with them both. They liked it. I had an orgasm. We all did. But afterwards I was afraid they'd talk, that they were laughing at me and saying I was queer. So at the first opportunity I went to the filing room with the girl and I had her because then they would know I was all right really."

Significantly, the one job he made something of a success at was in a firm which did not employ many attractive young men. Thus we see that in those deliberate acts of self-display which first suggested this line of investigation, Paul was at one and the same time demonstrating his heterosexuality and indulging his homosexuality. He is primarily homosexual, but his fear of being despised or laughed at because of this attraction has driven him to a complex pattern of exaggerated and ruinous heterosexuality. The only time he really enjoys heterosexual intercourse is when he can share the girl with another man, or can simultaneously observe a man. This is why intercourse never satisfies him. It is a substitute, undertaken to prove what an adventurer he is, that he is heterosexual.

Paul's satyriasis, then, is completely false, a constantly reiterated lie both to the world and to himself. His homosexuality was obviously fostered, as a child, by his fatherlessness, and by his close identification with his mother. Thus the normal process was reversed when the stepfather came on the scene. The stepfather's masculinity was strange and interesting because of his familiarity with his mother. Undoubtedly he fell in love with his stepfather and acted this love out with his uncle. The removal of the uncle equated to the loss of a lover. He saw himself as constantly rejected. This explains why he took so much notice of his friend's tirade against masturbation and homosexuality. Had he persisted in his desires, he knew that he would lose his friend. This he could not bear and so he was led into substitutional, heterosexual, behaviour, sharing his first and many subsequent girls with his friend and others whom he observed during the act.

He developed a strong and abiding aversion to masturbation. Not only did he believe that it exacerbated his homosexuality, but it was also a symbol of his direct homosexual experiences. Therefore it must be denied and he never took relief by masturbation despite his persistent, frustrated erections. That Paul believed intensely in the power of heterosexual intercourse as a protection against and denial of homosexuality is demonstrated by his seeking out prostitutes and coupling with them as often as possible. More important than the world, represented by his employers, colleagues and especially the men who surprised him in intercourse, was himself. He had to prove, over and over again and as often as possible, that he was heterosexually normal.

Paul V was led to understand the true nature of his problem and many of his fears concerning homosexuality were allayed. What persisted was a feeling that he would never find real love and affection from another male and although many of his homosexual inhibitions have been removed, he still frequents women. His satyriasis has disappeared, but he is now showing signs of becoming a classic bisexual, using both sexes indiscriminately in his search for love and admiration.

We can say, then, that there are two main categories of satyrs. The strictly heterosexual who use sex as a bolster to their egos and as a means of confirming their identities, and those, like Paul V, who are bisexual but stress their heterosexuality unreasonably in an attempt to deny their homosexual urges. There are, of course, many smaller groups contained within these major categories. Satyriasis is as destructive as nymphomania. Indeed, because it so often affects other, apparently unconnected areas of life, *e.g.* Paul's work, it is often more obviously and immediately destructive. It results in the same nervous exhaustion as nymphomania, but it is generally easier to assist. This is, of course, because although it is a serious and dangerous condition, it is fundamentally more superficial. In cases of satyriasis it is seldom necessary to deal with deeply complex emotions. It is a question, more often than not, of misdirected or repressed sexuality, whereas nymphomania is always rooted in some diffuse and damaging emotional complex.

CHAPTER 8: THE BISEXUAL IN LITERATURE

Until recently, bisexuality has been a completely taboo subject. Even the strictest societies of the past have been forced, in one way or another, to acknowledge the existence of sex and inevitably of the "forbidden vices", lesbianism and homosexuality. Yet the fact that a man or woman can enjoy both sexes has always been well hidden and firmly pushed to the back of the mind. An acknowledgement of homosexuality, in the general sense of the word, of course, enables people to confirm their own normalcy by contrast. The fact that *some* men and women prefer their own sex to the opposite has often been regarded, by hypocritical societies, as confirmation of its superiority. Of course, attitudes to the subject are always ambivalent, but it is a fact that, by and large, the man or woman who acknowledged homosexuality in others did so in order to make themselves feel better. This acknowledgement was, in other words, completely negative, a rejection of such "foul practices" which also served to salve their own consciences about their heterosexual indulgences. Homosexuality, then, regrettably existed, but only as something that other people did.

On the other hand, the very aspect of bisexuality which makes it possible for bisexuals to resign themselves to their nature, *i.e.* the fact that the "sin" of homosexuality is cancelled out by the "acceptability" of their heterosexual liaisons, has worked against its general admission. People on the whole, and particularly those living in very repressive societies, prefer to consider the existence of exclusive homosexuality as a deplorable but remote habit than to believe that the normal and accepted can be tainted by the depraved and forbidden. It is for the same reason, of course, that the bisexual has frequently been lumped indiscriminately together with the homosexual. Basically, bisexuality has been unacknowledged, even unthinkable, because it shatters carefully maintained illusions. To reject homosexuality of any kind is easy, but if one man or woman be capable of enjoying both sexes sexually, then who can hope to escape taint? Bisexuality hits too close to home, touches thoughts and dreams in the most sexually balanced person that they have always sought to repress.

Yet there is one area of life where bisexuality has flourished and has been seen to flourish. This is, of course, in erotica. Yet there is no mention of the term in any erotic book that has come to our notice, nor is there likely to be. Yet bisexual behaviour has become one of the clichés of erotica, second only to the tirelessly supersexed hero and the insatiable heroine. The reason for this is immediately obvious. It has always been difficult for the author of erotica to find means of presenting variety in his books. Difficult as it often is to believe, the endless repetition of scenes of sexual intercourse quickly palls, on both the reader and the writer. Diversity, variety is the very stuff of erotica, and one of the basic ways in which this may be obtained, from a literary point of view, is by the inclusion of various scenes of homosexuality. It is obvious that the hero who has a taste for his own as well as the opposite sex creates an opportunity for imaginative and varied scenes and thus widens the scope of the novel or story and simultaneously makes the task of holding the reader's attention much, much easier.

It may be thought, however, in spite of our remarks so far, that bisexual behaviour is a comparatively new element in erotic fiction, that the authors of the past were content to find variety by the inclusion in their works of many different women of varying ages and types. Perhaps they could have achieved their ends in this way, but the fact remains that they did not. On the contrary, bisexual behaviour abounds. We have, for example, only to think of that extraordinary monument of Victorian literature, *Walter - My Secret Life** to recall ample evidence there. Or if this does not convince the sceptic, the following extract from the privately published *Memoirs of Erotic Delights*, dated 1847, and purporting to be based on extracts from the personal confessions of Sir Clifford S, will serve as well as many other examples to prove our point.

Sir Clifford, with the aid of his lascivious mistress, Mrs Spendmuch, has succeeded in seducing the lovely Julia Fainall. True to the conventions of erotica, the newly debauched heroine takes to these new pleasures with an insatiable lust — with the following results.

"At length Sir Clifford rose and withdrew his tired engine from between the marbled thighs of his lovely conquest. 'Nay, sir, you'll not abandon her yet,' cried Mrs Spendmuch indicating the lady's yet palpitating charms which were quite exposed by her abandoned posture. 'Indeed, madam, a man can only do so much,' replied Sir Clifford. 'But truly, Sir Clifford,' cried the panting object of their converse, 'I have not done yet. Truth I have not.' 'But I am done, lady,' replied Sir Clifford, indicating his wilted weapon. 'Fie, what is to become of me?' cried Julia, wriggling her haunches on the bed. 'I shall go mad if I be denied.' 'Nor you shall,' said Mrs Spendmuch, placing herself between Julia's delicious legs and lustfully seizing her throbbing parts. 'For when men fail, a lady must needs look to her own sex.'

"Mrs Spendmuch's touch occasioned a renewed beating of the lady's body on the bed. All her charms jiggled in

---

* *Walter - My Secret Life*, 2 Vols., Luxor Press, London, 1967; also *More Walter*, Morntide, London, 1970.

rhythm to the practised hand of the older women who, in her turn, was seized by a veritable sweeping lust. Sir Clifford watched with regained interest as his mistress approached her face to the scarlet parts of his conquest and began there to tease with her tongue and full red lips what she had already delighted with her fingers. 'Oh... oh,' sighed Julia, thrusting her body forwards to meet the tantalising tongue. 'I spend... I spend.'

"The sight of this tribadic union greatly excited Sir Clifford who drew close to the bed, the better to observe the ministrations of Mrs Spendmuch on that precious sheath that had so recently held the very root of his manliness. This same object now became fired by the spectacle and began again to lift its head. Slipping his hands beneath the busy tribade's petticoats, he found that moist and quivery spot just as Julia reached the very height of her ecstasy. 'Ah!' cried she, only to be echoed by Mrs Spendmuch who, raising her head from its work, called, 'Ah, Sir Clifford, put it in me I beg, or I shall be forced to do meself.'

"The lusty man required no further invitation. Mrs Spendmuch rolled over and threw up her skirts. Her plump thighs rested on the edge of the bed, her head lay close to that part of Julia she had so recently pleasured while her charms were most meaningfully displayed to Sir Clifford who, nothing loath, seized his manly organ and buried it within the writhing lady."

Thus we have a classic example of bisexual behaviour. Sir Clifford has intercourse with both women who also have a lesbian connection. Mrs Spendmuch's behaviour cannot but be considered bisexual. Yet, of course, we must remember that lesbianism, the less prohibited of the two forms of homosexuality, has always been regarded as an acceptable part of the male sexual fantasy of which erotica is perhaps the supreme manifestation. The observation of lesbian acts, in other words, has always been an acceptable visual aphrodisiac for men, who are both the authors and major readers of erotica. The depiction of lesbianism in erotic books cannot be said to touch the reader, unless she be a woman. Yet the fact remains that the women presented in these books are invariably bisexual.

Perhaps it is even more startling that male homosexuality is also featured in these books, not as a separate incident but as an integral variation of the erotic theme. There is, of course, a famous homosexual scene in the complete edition of John Cleland's *Fanny Hill*, but it is not so much a part of the action as, for example, the following extract from *Realistic Pleasures*, another piece of Victorian erotica which is studded with male homosexuality. The baronet whose story it purports to tell has as much fondness for his page's bottom as for his many ladies' vaginas. At the end of the book the page's own story is told. The boy, at the age of sixteen, witnessed a number of vigorous love-making bouts between his mother and her lover, a colonel. The boy manages to seduce his mother in his own turn and these erotic delights are soon lent variety by the Colonel himself.

"The Colonel had for some time past been in the habit of calling me to him and making me sit close to him on the sofa, passing his arms round my waist and pressing me close to him, kissing me, and telling he loved me as a son. I suspected his affection was more erotic than paternal, for I saw by the bulging of his trousers that this always excited him. The sight of his standing pego had the same effect on mine and I saw that he always noticed this. On one occasion my mother had her dressmaker with her and he had to wait before he could see her. He drew me to him as usual and glided his tongue within my mouth and begged me to suck it. I did so and we were in a state of furious erection almost immediately. 'My dear boy,' said he, 'I see you are affected in the same manner as I am by these sweet embraces and you seem to be grown more than I could have thought for your age,' at the same time placing his hand on my throbbing pego. 'But nothing to your own, Sir,' said I. 'Would you like to see it?' said he. 'Above all things.' 'Well then you may unbutton me if you like while I do the same for you.' Out burst our two weapons. I took his and handled it with much enjoyment. He then rose and locked the door and begged me to lower my trousers and stand before him. He rubbed my bottom and gently frigged my staff and then stooping took it in his mouth, tickling the point with his tongue in the most delicious manner, at the same time contriving to frig the root with one hand. He suddenly lifted his head and inserting a finger in his mouth moistened it well. He then renewed his sucking and frigging and when he felt I was approaching the climax, he pushed his hand behind and put his moistened finger up me, and pushed it in and out in unison with his frigging and sucking, making me spend with more delight than I had ever yet experienced with Mamma. He sucked all out and only stopped when not a drop remained. He raised his head and asked me how I liked it. I told him the pleasure I had experienced and begged he would allow me to suck him. He allowed me to do so for a few moments, but would not spend as he said he had other work to do. He said I must come to see him, but not tell Mamma, on any account, anything about it."

In isolation, such a passage might well be taken as a quotation from a piece of exclusively homosexual erotica. But elsewhere in the book are found graphic descriptions of both the boy and the Colonel indulging heartily and joyfully in heterosexual activities. Bearing out our remarks concerning the use of bisexuality as a device for the depiction of variety, the book ends with a scene of troilism in which the youth enjoys the Colonel while the latter makes love to "Mamma". Unlike lesbianism, homosexuality is not genuinely believed to feature in the average masculine fantasy. On the contrary, the reader of heterosexual erotica is thought to have an antipathy to the very idea of homosexuality, yet the inescapable fact remains that very, very few books of this kind do not include some homosexual acts, albeit generally in a heterosexual group situation.

Thus, while held to be unthinkable in real life, bisexual behaviour has flourished in erotica. We must understand at once that the distancing principle is here again at work. The reader of *Realistic Pleasures* would certainly not buy and read with enjoyment a piece of purely homosexual erotica. He is not homosexual and most probably deplores and condemns those who are. Yet he happily accepts homosexual acts in erotic fiction and we may suppose that they add to his pleasure when reading the book. They do so because they do not threaten or impinge upon him. The devious human mind is quite capable of identifying completely with the hero when he is performing with some avid lady, but will put itself in the role of an interested observer during the homosexual scenes. Or, at least, this is how the reader will justify his reading of these passages, if he does not claim to have skipped them altogether. But, in fact, it is more than likely that he shares the hero's delight at this novel variation as much as he enjoys the heterosexual goings on. The great attraction of erotica is that it provides the reader with the illusion of participating in or witnessing acts which he would not normally entertain. The erotic novel holds a distorting mirror up to life. The world it creates is one blissfully free of the strictures, codes, *mores* and prohibitions of the real world. Literally anything is permissible, and the reader is transplanted into a world which mirrors and perhaps rivals his wildest fantasies. He indulges innocently in them, for no matter how closely he identifies with the characters and events of the book, he can always avoid the guilt and disgust which would most probably result if he were actually to do these things, by reminding himself that they are, after all, just a fiction, fundamentally unreal.

Today, however, it is widely thought that erotica's true attraction lies in the fact that it mirrors the unspoken desires of the reader. We have only to consider for a moment the abundance of flagellation in Victorian novels and stories to see how closely and accurately erotica embodies the preoccupations of the age in which it is written. The production and sale of erotica is a purely commercial business, and the authors thereof have always had to be sensible of the fact that their success depended solely upon their ability to give the public what it required. Thus in an age which saw flagellation as the supreme sexual occupation, it was unthinkable that it should be left out if the author wished to make money. Consequently, we can trace flagellation, in Victorian erotica, on its popular progress from an isolated variation to the point where it dominated the action to the virtual exclusion of all "normal" sexual activity. Yet even here, in these hymns to the buttocks and the birch, the bisexual element is discernible. Again there is a movement from books about men who whip women to a general *mêlée* in which women whip girls and men discipline boys. Although it is fair to say that each author had his preferred activity, we soon note the emergence of the tireless rod-wielding hero who gets as much pleasure from whipping his own sex as he does from chastising women. Nor, significantly, is there any difference in the reactions experienced by these characters as a result of the sex of their victims. It is a commonplace for a female flagellant to comment ecstatically on the shape and texture of the female buttocks, much as it is for a man to enthuse about the muscular rotundities of some luckless member of his own sex. And the outcome of these whippings is always intense sexual arousal, enjoyed by the instigator indiscriminately, no matter what the sex of the recipient.

It is, of course, this need to reflect the reader's interests, to provide what the customer wants, that causes the writers of erotica to produce books which are specifically concerned with some particular fetish or deviation. In these books, the question of range and variety is not nearly so important. If the reader's abiding interest is in gloves, then a constant repetition of detailed descriptions of beautiful hands in tight leather gloves is sufficient to secure the interest and to satisfy. Consequently, the bisexual element is scarce. The author is severely limited by his subject. He might be able to risk describing, say, a pair of masculine gloves, but any more concrete evidence of bisexuality in these specialised books is not possible. Books about male homosexuality, of course, are written for and read by homosexuals. Very few devotees of erotica will be interested in these, largely because they are inhibited by the social reaction to the subject. It is one of the mysteries of human behaviour that a man will happily read of homosexual connections and presumably even enjoy them, in predominantly heterosexual erotica, but will shun the exclusively homosexual which contains similar descriptions. Books dealing with lesbianism are, of course, another matter. A small body of frank, lesbian erotica is written for men. It appeals to the man, and there are many with such tastes, whose sexual imagination is fired by the idea of two or more women having sexual relations with each other. Books aimed specifically at lesbians themselves are seldom erotic and consequently of little interest to men. They are romantic, idealised stories which aim to reassure the lesbian, to fulfil the function of the romantic stories contained in women's magazines and which are enthusiastically read by heterosexual women.

But if we regard erotica as a literary convention which had to reflect accurately, albeit in terms that are larger than life, the sexual concerns of the majority, and we consider simultaneously that bisexual behaviour has always been a basic component of erotica, we are faced with a very interesting and revealing supposition. If we leave aside lesbianism because we must accept that the majority of readers are men and that to the average man the prospect of two women making love to each other is exciting, we are faced with the ambivalent popularity of homosexual acts in erotic fiction. If the readers had found these unpleasant or unecessary, we can be sure that the commercially concerned authors and publishers would have removed them. But they are, if anything, becoming more frequent and more detailed. Yet they are read, admittedly in a general heterosexual content, by men who regard themselves as sexually "normal" and who usually viciously condemn any form of male homosexuality and greatly fear any suggestion that they might find pleasure in such acts in any form. We have, in fact, a dramatic schism between the frequency and consistent appearance of these scenes in erotica and the supposed feelings of the readers.

There are, in fact, several principles at work here, or several methods of distancing which makes these literary homosexual acts acceptable. Most commonly, the acts are found to be acceptable because they occur in a general heterosexual context. The same motives apply here as those which persuade the man or woman in group sexual situations that homosexuality, male or female, is permissible under the special circumstances. The heroes of these books are always presented as heterosexual to an impossibly exaggerated degree. Thus the male reader identifying with this sexual superman can comfort himself with the belief that his homosexual diversions are "all right" because of his preceding and following heterosexual prowess. In other words, the law of cancelling out applies in fiction as much as it does in life. Others react more wholeheartedly to erotica. The fantasy world of forbidden acts and sexual impossibilities effectively "freezes" the readers' normal reactions, beliefs, etc. Thus he accepts the homosexual element as a logical part of the general orgy. Some men, of course, react actively to the homosexual passages, working on the revenge principle. These reactions are deliberately induced in some books where the hero (heterosexual, of course) uses a passive homosexual roughly and largely to "punish" him. This is the most disturbing reaction of all, and men who share this semi-sadistic feeling of triumph are usually latently homosexual themselves. But again the events are distanced, and whatever the quality and kind of positive reaction, the reader is always guilt-free because he knows it is only fiction, that he would never *really* do such things.

But all these reactions, which are often very skilfully played upon by the successful author, are evidence of bisexuality. This does not, of course, mean that all the men who accept and read the homosexual passages in heterosexual erotica are practising bisexuals or that they will become so. However, these reactions, and the popularity of such passages does indicate the truth of the point we made at the very beginning of this book, *i.e.* that all men and women are, to a certain degree and in a certain sense, bisexual. For we may be sure that heterosexual women reading the lesbian passages in these books will have a similar reaction pattern. The most positive aspect of erotica is that it acts as a release. It permits, for an hour or so, the reader to have the illusion of realising not only his wildest dreams, but dreams and wishes that lie dormant and unrecognised in his subconscious. To simplify, in other words the homosexual passages we have been discussing appeal to the repressed, partially developed feminine aspect which exists in the most adjusted and well balanced heterosexual man. Such escape valves are necessary. The scenes release emotions and reactions which are normally quite repressed in a guilt-free, harmless way. Such men, or women for that matter, are seldom, and certainly not necessarily, even dimly aware of these ambivalent wishes, nor is there any reason why they should be. The release is found in erotica and the tension is dissipated in this "passive" and harmless way. Faced with an actual opportunity to participate in homosexual acts of the kind he can enjoy reading about, such a man would probably be disgusted and impotent. His homosexual urge is very weak, but even so it requires the occasional, temporary acknowledgement which erotica can effectively provide. And so we see why bisexuality has always been instinctively used as a major theme in successful erotica, even when any public or official acknowledgement of the subject was completely unknown. It is basic to human nature, an inevitable part of the libido, but fortunately only the few are constained to practise it outside the fantasy world of fiction.

Let us now look at a passage from a piece of contemporary American erotica and try to analyse from this the probably reactions of the "average" reader, or rather those the author has aimed to create in his readers.

"I had been so busy necking with Laura, real deep tongue-to-tongue soul kissing, and I'd got my hand up under her sweater and was rolling her nipple between my fingers, that I hadn't thought to check what kind of progress Don and Ella had been making. Anyway, when I came up for air, I got the shock of my life. Ella's skirt was up around her hips and her panties were just a crumpled ball on the floor. From the way she was sitting, legs hooked up on the edge of the chesterfield and spread real wide, I should have been able to see everything, but Don's big head was in the way. He was down on his knees and I could tell from the far-off look on Ella's face and the moans she was making deep in her throat, her breasts heaving, that Don was giving her one hell of a tongue job.

"Seeing that really turned me on, and I nudged Laura and watched her eyes pop out of her head when she got a look at the action across the room. I had my hand up her skirt at once, and asked her if she would like for me to do that to her. 'Oh Ronald, would you really?' she cooed. I met with no resistance when I started in skinning off her panties, and I dove down there to give her a real work out. Man, in three minutes she was joggling and thrashing about so that I knew she was ready to go off. So I let up, and suggested we made for the bedroom and finished things off in style.

"Laura was so sex-weak I practically had to hold her up, but I paused by Don and Ella and invited them to get with it. They didn't need asking twice either, and what followed was a really wild scene. Ella, my kid sister, stretched out with every nook and cranny of her cute little well-stacked body showing beside Laura, all long and slim with those great juicy breasts rising up. Don and I were having a visual feast as we wrestled our way out of our pants and jockey shorts and dove onto the bed, onto all that luscious girl flesh. We lay beside the girls and finger worked them for a minute or two, but everybody's eyes were everywhere. Ella could scarcely get her hand around Don's hunk of manhood. I'd never have guessed he was so big.

"But now both girls were ready and we climbed on and both of us threw ourselves into the frenetic rhythm of bashing hell out of those moaning broads...

"We lay pacefully then, occasionally touching, looking at our sex used bodies. 'Hey, Laura,' said Ella, 'didn't I tell you Ron was an o.k. guy?' 'Sure,' Laura smiled at me, 'He's just like his sister.' 'Laura!' Ella screeched. 'What the hell does that mean?' Don wanted to know. Ella sat bolt upright on the bed. 'Laura Cameron, if you breathe another word, I'll... I'll...' 'Shut up,' I said, coming the big brother bit. 'Come on, Laura. Give,' I added. 'Oh nothing,' said Laura. 'Just that good bed performance seems to run in the family.' Slowly it dawned on us. Don and I exchanged wondering, meaningful looks. My throat had gone tight and dry again. 'You mean... er... Laura? You mean you've partied with Ella?' Laura smiled like a cat that had got the cream. 'Sure I have, haven't we honey?' She turned on her long flank and touched Ella's breast. 'You wanna see, boys?' 'Let go of me, Laura, you bitch,' shrieked Ella, but too late. Don forced her shoulders back onto the bed, and Laura started in working on her breasts and down between her thighs. Don stifled Ella's protests with a wet smacky kiss, and then Laura twisted round to put her tongue where her fingers had been. When Don pulled up for a look, Ella was crooning like a happy baby.

" 'Oh Laura. Yes. Like that. Oh, give it to me, baby. Harder,' she moaned. 'Shift over, you big mutt,' Laura said to Don, who obediently scrambled over Ella's body to perch next to me. In a second, Laura had straddled Ella's head with her thighs and the two girls were sixty-nining like mad. My eyes were bulging out of my head. 'Will you look at 'em go?' muttered Don. I glanced at him. The spectacle had produced a very obvious reaction in both of us. 'Oh man, that's too wild,' he said. 'Hey, Ron, I'm gonna go off again.' I knew how he felt, but when he reached over and grabbed me, I felt kind of funny. 'Hey,' I said, folding my hand around his. 'Not there, dope,' he grinned, 'grab a handful of this.' I looked from his rampant manhood to the girls. They sure didn't need any help from us. To cut in now would have been to blow the party, but like Don, I was crazy for it. I reached out and grabbed, started working on his joint just like he was doing to me.

" 'Hey baby,' he said, staring bug-eyed at the wildly thrashing girls, 'how about a bit of that action?' I guess I didn't think too much about it because Don fitted his actions to his words and the touch of his mouth on me really grabbed me where I live. I flipped over onto my side which brought me in line with his woman-killer. I didn't think I'd be able to manage that much, but what the hell, I thought, nothing ventured, nothing gained. After all, Don wasn't exactly chewing on a matchstick. So, with my eyes glued on Ella's darting tongue working Laura over, I opened my mouth and returned Don's compliment."

True to the pattern of erotica, this scene, which involves four American high school teenagers, moves from the common to the bizarre. Even from this edited version, we can grasp that the preliminaries of foreplay are carefully established between the two couples. The preponderance of oral sex acts is another example of the way in which erotica mirrors the preoccupations of the time, for today oralism is a major sexual concern, particularly in the U.S.A. However, the reader's reactions are what concern us and this passage ably demonstrates the way in which they are controlled by the author.

By using the device of the first person narrator, the author automatically ensures that the reader will identify easily and at once. In the early stages of the scene, two reactions are induced simultaneously. The narrator's personal tactile and emotional reactions are communicated directly and "shared" with the reader, while his periodic observation of the other couple adds a distanced visual stimulus. The visual stimulus predominates when the girls lie naked side by side on the bed, and an extra *frisson* is added by the fact that one of the girls is the narrator's sister. Thus, apart from sharing in the sight of two nude girls, the reader, because he identifies with Ronald, shares the "forbidden" thrill of an incestuous connotation. The first hint of homosexuality comes when Ronald remarks on the size of Don's penis. This is, however, firmly in a heterosexual context and, in any case, male genital organ size is accepted and not regarded as necessarily threatening. The passage describing the dual intercourse has been cut, but it contains again a mixture of tactile sensations (Ronald's) transferred direct to the reader via identification and, again, the remote stimulus of Ronald's observation of the other couple.

The lesbian element is, of course, presented entirely as a visual, observed act. It is important to note, however, that Ella's resistance, albeit if only token, is very important. This establishes the unusual nature of the act, *i.e.* it is not something which automatically happens, but her resistance is overcome by the eagerness of the others. Thus her blame or guilt is shared and therefore lessened. The male reader, eager for this scene and probably quite unconcerned as to its propriety, is none the less reassured. This reassurance is important, not in direct relation to the lesbian act itself, which is remote from a man in any case, and not widely regarded as prohibited, but as part of a softening up process which sets the scene for the homosexual element. Here it is established from the first that the homosexual act is only undertaken out of need, and to further reassure the reader, it is Don, not the narrator with whom he (the reader) identifies, who is the instigator. Thus Ronald's, *i.e.* the reader's, guilt is effectively lessened from the start. Furthermore, Ronald makes it quite clear that to interrupt the girls' pleasure would be ungallant, and would probably ruin the whole atmosphere. Again it is Don who begins to fellate him, and it is the friendship principle which clinches his participation. It would be, the implication is, churlish of him not to reciprocate. And, significantly, the image of Laura and Ella in their lesbian situation is fixed firmly in the reader's mind at the moment Ronald begins to fellate Don. This is particularly important because it distracts the reader's attention from his probable revulsion at the thought of taking a penis into his mouth, and also suggests that the erotic stimulus is not the homosexual act itself but the observation of the girls. Were Ronald to be shown to enjoy the homosexual act for itself, the reader would probably be alienated. As it is, his critical feelings can be directed at Don, the instigator of these events, while he can safely identify with Ronald whose actual participation is presented not in terms of homosexual enjoyment, but as a result of need, kindness and arousal as a result of watching the girls. These three factors make it "safe" for the reader to identify and to enjoy without feeling guilt, revulsion or any disturbing interest in homosexuality. And, of course, the whole incident is set in an atmosphere of intense permissiveness, of lust run riot in a world where the normal laws, moral and ethical, do not apply.

Today, erotica is becoming more and more concerned with bisexuality, the "two-way swingers" as the Americans call them, being a requisite feature of any successful book. And, at the time of writing, there seems to be every indication that this trend will develop and continue, that literary bisexuality will flourish. The main reason for this is, of course, that the authors are again having to provide the consumer with what he wants. At the moment, the concern is with permissiveness, with the casual freelove of the hippy movement. So much is written and said about permissiveness that it is easy to lose sight of the fact that the real permissives are still a small but undoubtedly significant minority. Their publicity, through little fault of their own, is so great that we tend to forget that the vast majority of people still believe in, are still subject to the stricter laws of a long established social morality. To these people, permissiveness has become the fantasy nirvana. The lurid and generally inaccurate newspaper reports of permissive goings on have fired the average imagination to such an extent that the hippy cult and permissiveness in general have become synonymous with the ultimate in sexual freedom. The authors of erotica which, as a result of the permissive phenomenon, has become less taboo and more openly, therefore more widely, in demand, have been quick to see in these genuine social trends the opportunity to provide their readers with a variety of sexual couplings without losing the tenuous link with verisimilitude that is essential to all fantasies. And simply because the hippies are headline news, their exaggerated depiction in erotic fiction is an immediate commercial attraction. For example:

"Rose, dressed only in three strings of quite beautiful Mexican beads which looped around and nestled between the perfect orbs, rose-tipped and slightly tilted, of her marbled bosom, clung tightly to Hank's arm as her eyes grew accustomed to the gloom and enabled her to see sights she had not even read about, let alone imagined. She tore her eyes away for a moment to glance at Hank, but his inevitable relaxed smile told her nothing.

"Suddenly a small, darkly beautiful Indian woman detached herself from the writhing *mêlée* of flesh and came towards them. Her bones were delicate, her skin coffee-gold, and she was nude except for a clashing orchestra of bangles about her fragile wrists. Delicate silver bells were knotted into her flowing black hair. Her mouth curled in a smile as she extended her arms in greeting. Her eyes were so large, so black that Rose thought they might, at any moment, spill over and engulf her face.

" 'Hank,' she cooed in a soft dove voice. 'How lovely. You've brought your friend.' And catching one of Rose's moist hands in hers, she added, 'How beautiful you are. Hank told us, but we could not believe. Now you see how the doubters are converted.' Clasping Rose's wrist firmly, she began to pull her gently, but insistently, into the fleshy crowd. Rose hung back, threw a helpless look at Hank, but he merely pushed her in the small of her back, propelling her forward. The press of bodies, of naked, sweating, sexually striving bodies was suddenly thick around her. Helplessly she looked for Hank, but the woman slipped an arm around her waist and drew her suddenly close. So close that Rose saw her heavy purple nipples brushing against her own rose-flushed skin.

" 'You are so beautiful, so remotely beautiful that I feel I should take you straight to Ali, my husband, but I cannot find it in me to make such a sacrifice. I shall keep you, beautiful girl, for myself.' So saying the woman lodged her bird-claw fingers into the tender spot that previously only Hank had ever entered. 'Oh-ooh!' sighed Rose. 'But... but Hank? I really ought to...' She twisted and turned, her full breasts brushing against the powerful chest of a bronzed god who happened to be passing. A strange, unidentified hand clasped her buttocks. She shivered and wriggled. 'Nonsense, my dear,' cooed the Indian lady with the disturbing fingers. 'Hank brought you here so that we might get acquainted.'

"Rose was about to speak through the sexual haze that seemed to rise up and stifle her when the woman disappeared, literally, as though a trap-door had opened beneath her. 'The wages of sin!' Rose told herself sagely, when familiar bird-like hands forced open her thighs and a similarly-bird-like tongue began to tickle her just as Hank had done. Before her bones quite turned to water, Rose peered down into the shadows. The tiny Indian woman was kneeling between her legs. Her nose, buried in the golden fuzz of Rose's lower stomach, made her seem as though she had acquired a beard.

"The sensations which swept through Rose completely disarmed her. She wondered if Hank had told this unusual lady how much she liked that tongue tickling. But just then a great rush of delight made her nearly overbalance, and flinging wide her arms with a cry of dismay, Rose was immediately caught and supported by two young men, two beautiful young men whose heads lay against her breasts and whose broad satiny shoulders now supported her arms. 'So kind,' smiled Rose gratefully before another wave gripped her. As though nodding acknowledgement, they dipped their heads and each scooped a precious pulsing nipple into their moist boyish mouths.

"At that moment a light came on, a dull green-blue glow at the end of the room which gave the figures it revealed a mysterious, dream-like quality. Through the fog of her delicious transports, (someone was now using a tongue behind!) Rose made out the unmistakeable lithe frame of her adored Hank. She thought his pose a little ungraceful, but she felt tender just seeing him again, her treasure, so close. But she squealed with fright and amazement when she saw what they were doing to her love, her boy. At first she thought they were hurting him, but from his ecstatic shout, the broad grinning flash of his white teeth, she decided he must like that man's big thing *there*. How strange, she reflected, are the ways of men, and how little she, a poor, mere, delicious girl, knew of them. But my goodness, she silently cried, even Hank could not want to eat that enormous lollipop. But he did, with a roar of pleasure which somehow became intermingled with Rose's own pleasure so that she felt her body bursting and flying apart to merge with her happily receiving, greedily gulping lover.

"A moment later the woman stood up and cuddled Rose with her arm again, brushing away the still nibbling boys. 'Now' she said, pressing Rose to her, 'I think we really know each other.' 'Oh yes,' said Rose. 'And I'm very pleased to make your... er... acquaintance.' Her troubled gaze turned again to her battered and gulping boy. The Indian woman followed the direction of her eyes. With a skip, she clapped her hands. 'Oh goody,' she chirruped, 'Hank's met Paul. I knew they'd get along.' 'Which is Paul?' said Rose, as delicately as she could. 'Why, the one who is about to give Hank his love-tribute,' said the Indian lady with a rapt expression on her face. Rose repeated her question, for both her lover's assailants seemed to be on the edge of shattering climaxes. 'Why, I see what you mean,' the woman nodded. 'Paul is in front, dear. Ali is behind. If you'll excuse the pun. You must meet Ali.

He won't be a moment. He's just saying hello to Hank.'"

Rose, another in the long line of eponymous heroines who have followed Candy, is an English innocent dropped into a multi-racial hippy community. In this extract we see the constant reiteration of the gentle, casual acceptance of sex. Making love is saying hello, and *vice versa*. Love is extended to all and is expressed in the most frankly sexual way. Although this element is exaggerated here for comic effect, it is, none the less, an acceptable mirror of permissive life. The bisexuality of all the characters is simply taken for granted. There is no need, in these books, for the author to persuade the reader into accepting homosexual acts. The hippy philosophy is love for everyone. Carried to its logically illogical conclusion this, of course, overrides sex barriers. Men love women, men and themselves. It is a classless, raceless, unisexual world. The reader's guilt is effectively allayed by the philosophy. He is free to regard these characters as freaks, as social misfits, or as the truly free and admirable, but whatever reaction he has, he is reassured by their adherence to a way of life which completely overthrows the usual, accepted taboos. In this idealised world, everyone is beautiful and everyone loves where the fancy takes them, irrespective of all considerations.

It is a chastening thought that erotica today has completely embraced the tenets of permissiveness. The socio-sexual revolution which is so much a mark of our time, is being popularised and spread by the dissemination of books like *Rose*. It is, of course, also true to say that erotica is exploiting an existing phenomenon and that this close connection between the two will undoubtedly harm the philosophy with a great many people. Yet it is natural that the two should go together. Sexual freedom, the destruction of outmoded taboos is the prime aim of the new philosophy and this naturally includes the frank acceptance of erotica. And the opportunities for imaginative writing on the hippy way of life, plus the subject's topicality, make permissiveness a natural peg for the authors and publishers of erotica. However, it will indeed be revolutionary if the new freedom succeeds through one of the organs of communication it has sought to free from repression and prohibition.

As with all erotica, the contemporary variety encounters little difficulty in the presentation of lesbianism. Today, the last vestiges of reticence have been blown away from this subject, and because the demand remains stable, lesbian acts continue to be featured in erotic books. But today, erotica encroaches closer than ever to life. We have only to think of the prevalence and popularity of wife-swapping to see that books like *Rose* and hundreds of others are much less fantastical than their equivalents of a hundred years ago. The incidence of lesbianism is also increasing as more and more heterosexual women indulge occasionally in this special source of pleasure. But if the presentation and reception of lesbian acts in erotic books remains pretty stable, it cannot be denied that homosexuality, which still presents something of a problem, is also becoming an essential part of the *genre* today. Of course, the permissive philosophy provides an admirable excuse for the author who wants to vary his book by the inclusion of male homosexual acts. The actual social attitude towards the subject, as we have frequently pointed out, is rapidly becoming more tolerant and, as we have also said, the doubtful reader can always exonerate himself by recalling that the characters in these books are not subject to the existing social *mores*, but have deliberately overthrown them. The accent is on *love*, and its expression with a member of the same sex is difficult to attack under these special circumstances. Indeed, as far as erotic fiction is concerned, homosexuality of some kind is essential if the character is going to claim to be a hippy. Frequently some sop is thrown to the disturbed reader. A favourite device is to present the hero as a theoretical permissive, a man who condones and encourages everything, but who remains strictly heterosexual in practice himself. The popular denouément of such books is the orgy in which the hero is persuaded to partake in homosexual acts, is forced, in fact, to prove that he believes what he says. The rueful, but smiling hero, always succumbs but his reactions are seldom dwelt upon. In this way the reader can enjoy the hero's discomfiture and the homosexual element without feeling threatened or directly involved. It simply serves him right for preaching what he did not practise.

There is, however, one further manifestation of male homosexuality in contemporary, primarily heterosexual erotica which is quite definitely peculiar to our time and which is rather more disturbing than any other examples we have looked at. It is, also, extremely revealing of our prevailing sexual attitudes. We are, in fact, referring to the enforced homosexual "rape" or "seduction" of the flagrantly heterosexual hero. On the surface, of course, it is reasonably convincing to accept these incidents as another reflection of the hippy philosophy which undoubtedly dominates contemporary erotica. The hero, or anyone come to that, is a "square", "non-swinger" unless he embraces all forms of sexuality, unless, to coin a phrase, he extends the arms of loving brotherhood to his own as well as the opposite sex. In other words, the heterosexual male is being shown just what he is missing, and in the books where this is indisputably the intention, the hero always acknowledges that he was wrong, while hastily retiring to the arms of his waiting mistress. However, this argument is not sufficient to justify the much more prevalent scenes in which the "straight" hero is "bent" a little, quite against his will.

An admirable example is to be found in another American publication which centres around the turbulent and incredibly sexual affair between Angelina, a super-swinger, and Frank, a reasonably "square" but sexually voracious Princeton graduate. Angelina is a mysterious figure, semi-hippy, semi-whore, she is much more sexually experienced than the rugged, handsome, rich hero. In fact, the formula of *Rose* and others of the *genre* has here been reversed with the man cast in the innocent role. Frank is, however, as we might expect, a willing pupil and he soon learns a number of new and bizarre sexual tricks from Angelina. When Angelina confesses her penchant for lesbianism to him, he takes it, as they say, like a man, *i.e.* he is delighted and curious. He happily observes Angelina performing lesbian acts with a girl friend, and later in the book joins in one of Angelina's lesbian parties. However, he is always reticent about homosexuality. In response to Angelina's constant probing, he insist that he knocked out the only man who ever dared to make a pass at him. But Angelina is fascinated by the idea of her lover being sodomised and performing fellatio. In group situations, she often tries to persuade him to have homosexual relations, but even though he knows he will please her by agreeing, Frank consistently refuses. And so Angelina arranges things her own way.

She gets Frank very drunk one evening and tantalises him by undressing but staying out of reach. She undresses him, and uses her wide repertoire of sexual arts to arouse him. Just, however, as he is about to possess her, half-crazy with postponed lust, two burly young men burst from their hiding places and overpower Frank. They strip, and while Angelina crows with triumph and delight, Frank is painfully sodomised. However, the constant sight of his mistress and the eventual pleasure he takes in the act make him a reasonably willing fellator. After this, at Angelina's instigation, he is made the slave of the two homosexuals who make him suffer every indignity for which he is eventually rewarded by being allowed to sodomise one of them before falling into her arms.

Such scenes, in this and many other contemporary books, have such obviously sadistic overtones that it is impossible for any reader to regard them as mild deviations from the fictional fantastical norm. Indeed, Angelina's behaviour throughout the book is dominating and selfish, traits which are most clearly revealed in the scene described above. They cannot be taken unequivocally and one would expect the heterosexual male reader to find the passages unacceptable. Yet by their prevalence and frequency, and by the undeniable success of books containing such passages, it is obvious that they do not, that they have a place in the reader's fantasy scheme of sexual things.

There are, basically, two reasons for this surprising fact. Firstly, the point that the hero is forced into these acts successfully distances them from the reader. Even if he responds positively while reading about them, he is protected by the fact that the hero behaves in this way against his will, to please the tormenting girl and by the fact that he is rewarded by access to the girl herself. Often the actual male rape occurs simultaneously to the hero having intercourse with the heroine, and thus the general heterosexual ambiance is firmly established. By this denial of the hero's will, the reader can also choose to ignore the passage if he wishes, but if he should identify with it then he can do so either on the revenge principle, by putting himself in the role of the active male, which "exonerates" him, or by placing himself in the will-less and therefore blameless position of the hero.

The second reason, however, is the more important and the more revealing. It is a fact that male masochism is the most successful theme of contemporary erotica. Books with this theme range from the complete fantasy, in which a man voluntarily subjects himself to impossible tortures and unbelievable indignities at the hands of a cruel, automaton-like woman, or the quasi-real, the certainly possible, such as the story of Frank and Angelina.

These latter books are not aimed at masochists *per se* but at the increasingly acknowledged masochist in all men. The stories are, basically, straightforward heterosexual erotica, but variety, a "twist", is added by the inclusion of male subjection to the will of an imperious woman. Surprisingly often this takes the form of enforced participation in homosexual acts, often of a painful and disgusting nature, to satisfy the heroine's whims.

It cannot seriously be doubted that this masochistic homosexual element appeals to a great many readers. It is, of course, an "acceptable" way of presenting homosexual acts since it neatly circumnavigates the usual heterosexual objections to the subject. But more importantly, it is a peculiarly effective way of punishing and degrading the victim. He has to bear not only his natural revulsion against sexual contact with his own sex and the indignity of being dominated, but also the genuine physical pain and emotional trauma of the situation. Undoubtedly this is often very appealing to the latent masochist in the reader and, of course, it is also further proof, as are all these examples, of the existence of the bisexual urge in virtually all of us.

To sum up, it is sufficient to reiterate that bisexual behaviour, although seldom ever the subject itself, is a dependable requisite of erotic literature. It is one of the few ways man has discovered of making the prohibited acceptable. Working on the principle that anything is permissible in a dream or fantasy, the successful author of erotica has always been quick and inventive in seizing his opportunities for indulging in as wide a range of sexual activities as possible without alienating the reader. Judged solely from this point of view, we cannot but feel that erotica has a beneficial influence. Granted that the homosexual urge exists even though repressed, latent or unknown, in all men and women, it becomes essential for this urge to be released and exercised from time to time. By reading books which include acceptable depictions of homosexual or lesbian behaviour, this is accomplished without harm to the reader or anyone else. And, as we have seen, as our knowledge of sex increases and our attitudes towards it become freer and healthier, so the embodiment of bisexual behaviour becomes more obviously stressed, more consciously presented and in greater detail. This is a trend which seems certain to continue and, in its small way, it will undoubtedly help to create a more relaxed climate for the bisexual himself and may well help him or her to resolve his own predicament. And, of course, we should not forget that these books have an obvious appeal to the practising bisexual who can respond wholeheartedly to all varieties of behaviour depicted. But then we must also remember that bisexuality is only an exaggerated form of our common, natural condition which the writers of erotic books instinctively understand, although we may prefer to forget it.

CHAPTER 9: THE BISEXUAL AND THE FUTURE

It is, of course, much to early to begin to evaluate accurately the long-term effects, if any, of permissiveness. But because the movement is so widespread and so eagerly accepted by young people, it seems certain that it will continue to flourish and develop. These people will not, after all, stay young for long and the suggestion that they will become less radical with maturity is one which displays more wishful thinking than truth. Today's permissives will be tomorrow's responsible citizens, but this does not necessarily entail that their attitudes to sexual freedom of expression will change. And so the code of permissiveness will be passed on to succeeding generations. The revolution will be a quiet and gradual one, but it seems inevitable that it will take place, for it embodies the important volume of work which has so greatly added to our understanding and knowledge of sexual behaviour.

Predictions are, of course, always hazardous, but within this context of a growing general reappraisal of sexual attitudes one can be reasonably certain that bisexuality will move towards a greater acceptance. So many factors contribute to a society's attitude to specific sexual behaviour that, in a sense, one cannot responsibly predict how flagellation, for example, will be regarded in ten years' time. But if we postulate a general relaxation of strictures as a result of permissiveness, we can see the emergence of various factors which should help towards a general acceptance of bisexuality.

The word "revolution" is a dangerous one. Not only is it violently emotional, but it has the effect of suggesting that all opposition will be ruthlessly swept away overnight. Permissiveness will not operate in this way. There will be, for many years to come, a strong opposition which will only gradually become accustomed to what amounts to a reversal of established reactions. This will not be accomplished overnight and we believe that bisexuality will be accepted more quickly than other forms of "exceptional" sexual behaviour simply because it is fundamentally less disturbing than many other genuine perversions. To the entrenched it will be the lesser of many evils, and negative as this may be, it will eventually help towards the acceptance of bisexuality.

The very illusions which people hold about bisexuality will contribute to this aspect of the acceptance process and will probably affect the general trend. As we have seen, bisexuals do not regard their homosexual behaviour as reprehensible simply because their heterosexual liaisons cancel out their homosexuality. A similar reaction is at work, as we have also seen, among the readers of flagrantly bisexual erotica. Usually, the illusions people hold about any "forbidden" sexual behaviour work to repress it, but in this case, the illusion is likely to increase the acceptance of bisexual behaviour. And when we consider that homosexuality is tolerated more and more we can surely accept that the stigma which has successfully driven the bisexual underground but which has never outlawed or persecuted him as cruelly as the exclusive homosexual, will be lifted to a much greater extent. Of course, even in these permissive days, it is impossible to imagine a time when homosexuality will be accepted as natural. The processes of sex are too fundamentally linked to procreation for this ever to become possible. But the man or woman who entertains an infrequent desire for his or her own sex will undeniably be affected by the new toleration of homosexual acts, especially since they can rationalise them in a context of heterosexuality.

A great many of the controversies between permissives and their detractors are based on fundamental misunderstandings. There are, of course, those who simply do not believe in sexual freedom for a complex variety of reasons, but such people are probably smaller in number than is generally believed. The real stumbling block encountered by non-permissives is their ingrained attitudes to sex as a necessary but basically unpleasant expression of love and affection. Most of these people have grown up in a world where sex was not openly discussed and where one's sexual feelings were directed, at least in theory, to one chosen partner. Promiscuity was the most feared, the dirtiest word in their vocabulary and, to these people, the permissives appear to be casually and animally promiscuous. This is a fundamental misunderstanding. Two facts have, more than any other, shaped and formulated the permissive sexual philosophy. The first, and perhaps the most important, is a non-hypocritical acceptance of the fact that man is not and never has been an exclusive emotional or sexual creature. No one, no matter how entrenched in a quasi-religious sexual upbringing, can honestly deny that men and women have not always been attracted to a number of people, and very few in number are those who can honestly say that they have known, in the sexual sense, only one partner. Lucky indeed is the individual who can love once and once only, who is temperamentally fitted to be faithful to one person, to be satisfied by sexual relations with one and one person only. Nor is such an individual a true representative of the norm. He or she should rather be regarded as an exception, an outsider to the general instincts of human beings. Thus the permissives are not really doing anything so very new or extraordinary. They are simply admitting that men and women "love" many people, are sexually attracted to a number of potential partners. By refusing to acknowledge any barriers to the expression of such emotions or sexual feelings they are doing nothing more shocking than to express this love *openly*. Established morality is such that it regards hypocrisy and secrecy as virtue. The only "shocking" thing the permissive does by acknowledging his fundamental nature is to admit it openly and honestly.

The second shaping factor which we must take into account in any consideration of the permissive philosophy is the belief in universal love. Love is put forward as the alternative to strife, and it has been assumed that the "love" meant was purely spiritual, more brotherly than erotic. Yet it is difficult to find any reference among the formulators of permissiveness to any such particularisation of what is intended by the word "love". Perhaps the truth is more accurately expressed by the slogan, "Make Love Not War". This, by and large, should be taken literally. It is a naive but appealing philosophy which simply states the fact that if people copulate they cannot be fighting. The tepid and fearful commentators of permissiveness, the eternal occupiers of fences, have propagated this idea of a universal non-erotic love. But the permissive, basing his beliefs on the coolly logical philosophies of the East, believes that if one loves one's neighbour it is natural and logical to express that love. Love, in the spiritual sense, should not be reserved for one person, for the "soul mate" of romantic fiction. Love should be a tender emotion, an attitude of mind perhaps best understood as a deep friendship which can be logically and acceptably expressed sexually if erotic feelings exist between any two individuals. Thus the embattled detractors need not fear that love is being sold down the river. Rather are they asked to accept that love is a word which has been improperly annexed to mean a certain spiritual/sexual feeling between a man and one woman. The permissives who sleep with many people are not behaving like animals with no care or consideration of other people but are merely expressing their genuine love for each and every one of these people.

In this context the bisexual becomes immediately acceptable. The permissive seeks to make unconditional an activity which has for centuries been hedged around with prohibitions and exceptions. To their credit, the permissives so far have shown themselves to be more logical than their forebears, for they have seen, to give but one example, that once one has accepted the idea of loving all one's neighbours, one cannot begin to make conditions about the sex of the loved one. This point has, indeed, been an effective device for distinguishing between the true permissive and the fellow traveller, many of the latter having baulked at the mere idea of extending physical love to their own sex. Others, like Jeanne M have been persuaded.

"Yes, I am a permissive. I believe in complete sexual and moral freedom. I do not understand how you can ever hope to get the best out of people if you always hem them in with rules and prohibitions. That way they cannot grow or hope to discover what is good in them. But like so many people, I regarded myself as strictly heterosexual. I felt the usual liberal tolerance and concern for the lesbian and the homosexual. I deplored their ostracism, the dirty jokes about them, and believed, as I still do, in their right to lead their own lives peacefully. But all that was nothing that directly concerned me. I liked men. Men excited me and I never saw this as anything that could be changed.

"Then I met a girl with whom I did a lot of voluntary work. She was someone I admired tremendously. She taught me a lot, and our ideas were very similar on most things. Then she suddenly made sexual advances towards me. I was shocked. I refused, and she accepted it without a fuss, but I could see that she was hurt. I couldn't forget the incident, even though she did nothing to remind me of it. She was still as kind and good to me as she had always been, but I sometimes saw a longing and a sadness in her eyes.

"I began to see that I had behaved stupidly, that by rejecting her in this way I had revealed myself either as a prude or as a hypocrite. But what disturbed me even more was the fact that I had rejected a part of her after she had been so marvellous to me. My feelings towards her, my estimation of her character were not changed by her sexual overtures. I realised, in fact, just how stupidly I had behaved, and I told her so. We made love together afterwards and I responded completely.

"I don't regard myself as a lesbian. Men are still my chosen sexual partners, but occasionally I meet a girl and there is some very special emotion between us and I'm perfectly relaxed about expressing it. I suppose this makes me bisexual, and if it does, then all I can say is that it is a perfectly natural state. I don't chase after my own kind. I don't dress or think like a man and don't seek out 'butch' women. Some women I like more than others and have learned that this liking can be expressed in sexual terms without any loss of pleasure or great crises of conscience. It is, to me, no different to going to bed with a man for the first time.

"I think most people feel that one lesbian experience makes you into a raving dyke. And similarly they think that a bisexual is someone who is forever trying to have sex with everybody in sight. But it's not like that. One has sex with people one chooses, just as everyone else chooses and sleeps with their partner. The only difference is that the partner might be a man or a woman."

This very honest account contains a lot of truth. Indeed it indicates the very crux of the controversy, *i.e.* whether it is better that people's full potential should be curtailed because the removal of inhibitions and prohibitions will result in "immoral" behaviour, or whether human beings should be free to express themselves as completely as possible. There is, of course, no easy answer and ultimately everyone must reach their own conclusions. However, in this confrontation one fact is constantly overlooked. That is that morality is not steadfast. In the mid-twentieth century the majority of people can clearly see that moral codes are not divinely formed and given, but that they are evolved by men for men. The catalogue of sins committed by men in the name of God are legion, but perhaps none is so wide-reaching in its repressive effects than the establishment and enforcement of an unrealistic morality without the potential for growth and adaptation. So confused are our attitudes to this vague subject of morality than we tend to lose sight of the fact that it is, in essence, a voluntary code erected not for the restraint and punishment of men but for their betterment. There was a time when the idea that by refraining from sexual indulgence a man made himself spiritually stronger was justifiable according to the beliefs of the day. But that time is long past and this attitude to sex is even more harmful today in the light of our increased knowledge than it has ever been. Furthermore, if we comprehend morality in this way, as a flexible measure for man's betterment, we see that any morality worthy of the name is as acceptable as another. Thus the permissive cannot be regarded as immoral any more than a primitive society which condones homosexuality or incest can be regarded as immoral. All we can say is that these other ways of behaving are immoral according to our code, but quite morally acceptable by theirs. We have no right to enforce our beliefs on another. Surely we know now, better than ever before, how horrifying the results of any such attempts can be.

Yet even if people can learn to regard morality in this light, they may well feel that it is better for man to enjoy only a limited sexual freedom, may maintain that freedom is best measured by the conditions to which it is subject. In matters of sex there are, indisputably, a great many people who believe that man does himself no good, is not in any sense "bettered" by being free to indulge his sexual nature to the full. Certainly it would be foolish to suggest that sexual freedom will automatically result in man's betterment, but that is not the point. The amazing and unsuspected discoveries about the role and function of human sexual expression over the last hundred years have shown us, beyond all reasonable doubt, that sex is central to man's existence, that sexual flaws and deviations affect and harm, limit and misdirect totally different areas of man's life. Thus we must understand that if we prohibit a certain desired mode of sexual behaviour, we can by no means be sure that we are not interfering with other aspects of life. If we prevent a man from expressing himself sexually in a way which seems natural and instinctive to him, we are, in all probability, preventing him from realising his full potential in other asexual fields. Furthermore, the limitation of sexual expression creates a concentration of energy which should rightfully be used in other aspects of life. Sex is central to life just as the heart is central to the body, yet one does not consider the heart and its functions unless something goes wrong. When sexual expression is repressed and limited, when the demands of the libido are consistently unsatisfied, sex occupies more time, uses up more energy than is either necessary or proper and this has a deleterious effect on other aspects of life. Sex is central but it should run smoothly, just as the heart does, but, in our present society, sex occupies too much time and energy. If freedom were granted there would be more time and effort put in to the betterment of man.

Jeanne M's remarks about the bisexual personality are also very pertinent and illustrate the point we have just made. In a sense, in this book we have run the risk of adding to the popular misrepresentation of bisexuality in so far as we have been forced, as all researchers are, to consider extreme cases. The bisexuals like Jeanne M do not come to our attention because they have no need of help or guidance. As always we must arrive at a portrait of the general from the particular. This does not mean, however, that bisexuality is an ideal sexual state, certainly not in our present society. But for every case which comes to the attention of specialists, there are many others, like that of Jeanne M, which are easily handled. In the Permissive Society, not as it exists at present but as it may one day become, the bisexual will become more and more balanced. His problems at present are invariably the result of personal and exterior prohibitions, but if these are effectively removed there is every reason to believe that the problems will also be removed. And in this connection it is important to stress what Jeanne M has already pointed out, *i.e.* that this will not result in a great upsurge of indiscriminate, promiscuous sexual behaviour. On the contrary, the bisexual will share his sexual favours with no more people than the heterosexual or the homosexual. He will differ only in the catholicity of his selection. Already many happily married bisexual men have come to our notice who occasionally, at irregular and often long intervals, permit themselves a sexual escapade with their own sex. Significantly, their infidelities are seldom perpetrated with the opposite sex, thus displaying the tendency among bisexuals to cancel out their socially condemned digression. These men argue that unfaithfulness with men impinges less upon their wives than it would if the new partner were a woman. And, of course, the fact that they are married cancels out any suggestion of their being truly homosexual. Thus we see that it is possible for the bisexual to lead a balanced and unremarkable life. The fact of his infidelity cannot be regarded as worse or more reprehensible because it is conducted with his own sex. In effect, he is behaving exactly like millions of other married men and this compromise position only underlines the truth of the permissive belief in natural non-exclusiveness in romantic and sexual relationships.

There are already contemporary phenomena which indicate, if not a spreading and acceptance of bisexuality, at least a general bisexual climate. The most obvious and perhaps the most telling of these is the current blurring of the masculine and feminine images. It is a commonplace today for people to mistake girls for boys and *vice versa*. Girls have shorn their hair and flattened their chests. Trousers, often ones made specifically for men, have become a necessary feature of feminine wardrobes. Shoes have become clumpish and masculine, when they are not replaced by boots. Men, on the other hand, have grown their hair to shoulder length. Their clothes have become colourful and softly feminine in style and cut. Lace and satin have been adopted by the male, as have frills and ornate accessories. So fundamentally interchangeable indeed are clothes between the sexes, that designers and manufacturers have coined the word "unisex" to describe a range of garments which are identical in cut, colour and style but made in both male and female fittings. To advertise this fashion phenomenon, London has recently been dotted with posters showing the lower bodies of two models, male and female buttocks encased in identical polka-dotted briefs. Even underclothes, that last bastion of fluffy femininity, have become unisexual. Now that girls have abandoned the brassiere and men have opted for colourful abbreviated underpants, the final blurring of the sexual image has taken place.

But unisex is not just a fashion gimmick. On the contrary, it is a shrewd move on the part of manufacturers and marketers to meet a public demand. For some time now girls have been buying men's clothes and, to a lesser extent, *vice versa*. Now it is possible for the same garments to be obtained for both sexes in the one shop. Unisex is a simple commercial rationalisation of a public demand. It is, however, dangerous to draw any inflexible conclusions from the unisex phenomenon and one must constantly be aware of the ease with which it is possible to over-interpret the evidence to fit a chosen argument. What is significant is that the accepted image of the sexes is no longer valued. The old concept of femininity, fussy, frilly and frail, and that of masculinity, colourless, ill-fitting, tweedy, have become laughable. They were, at best, an exaggeration of a very rigid concept of femininity and manliness. Today the accent is on beauty, on the natural lines of the human body, on a peacock-like decoration of a basic shape. But this gives rise to confusion and necessarily draws the sexes closely together. The differences between men and women have always been stressed, but today, as a result of the movement towards unity and brotherhood, these differences are played down.

It would, of course, be ludicrous to even suggest that all the followers of unisex fashion are bisexual. Nothing could be further from the truth. But this unisexual image does indicate the potential of bisexuality. There are those who will argue that by dressing in this way the individual is giving a symbolic acknowledgement to the opposite sex within. If this is so, and it is by no means proven, then it will effectively halt a rise in bisexual behaviour. But if it is not so, is, as we are inclined to believe, a natural trend which will create a general unisexual climate, then it is possible that it will create a situation in which bisexuality will flourish. The old images of masculine and feminine were based on mystery. The young man was curious and entranced by the mystery of what lay beneath those frothy petticoats and swirling skirts, just as the baggy squareness of men's clothes cloaked the comparable mystery of his body. But today, with improved and increased sexual education, young people are quite conversant with the anatomical differences and the mystery has been abandoned. Similarly, the relationship between the sexes has become more casual. Boys and girls can get along with each other as they are and the mystery of sex has been returned to its true home — the wonder of sexual expression. Thus with surface mystery removed, everybody is more or less equal and some of the subtlest embargoes to homosexuality have been removed. When mysteriousness was an occupational prerequisite of sex, one's own sex seemed dull and quite unmagical. But now that sex is regarded more casually, now that the psychological aspects of sex are taken more into account, the idea of mystery is not so important and either sex can be equally "different". Furthermore, as women have deglamourised themselves, so men have added glamour to their appearance. This is a climate which sets the scene for the breaking down of sexual barriers. This demystification and image blurring makes the exclusiveness of sexual opposites seem much less important.

When all is said and done, it is, of course, impossible to say where all this permissiveness and similar sexual image-making will end. Some people imagine that we are moving towards a bisexual Utopia in which sex will be a simple expression of human love and will be directed indiscriminately to both sexes. If such a world does come into existence, it will undoubtedly be a long time hence. The wish for such a Utopia is based upon a sensible desire to get sex in perspective. By surrounding it with barriers and prohibitions we force it out of focus, stress it in a way that is neither sensible nor healthy. But it is debatable whether such an extreme swing to freedom would be either acceptable or beneficial. People who put forward this argument generally have a vested interest and their motives should be regarded with some caution. The argument tends to overlook the fact that heterosexuality is not a convention of society, not a way of life dictated by churches and other authorities but the basic natural inclination of men and women. Heterosexuality will always continue to be paramount and exclusive homosexuals will remain a minority. But there is a growing feeling that too much has been made of heterosexuality, that simply because it is natural and desirable it has been unrealistically insisted upon to the detriment of other forms of sexual expression.

It is a popular misconception of Victorian thinking that the Greeks, the most overtly bisexual race of whom we have much information, were perverted. Today it is still claimed that "love" was reserved for members of like sex whereas heterosexual expression was reduced to the necessary but unfeeling mechanics of procreation. For some people this was undoubtedly true, but not for the majority. The Greeks were simply bisexual, a living proof of man's need to love several people, of his inevitable potential for bisexual behaviour. As we learn more and more about the existence of the opposite sex in each and every one of us, so the Greek idea of bisexual love becomes more and more persuasive and attractive, and perhaps the true outcome of our socio-sexual revolution will be a greater toleration of a similar state of sexual affairs.

Extremists on both sides tend to lose sight of the fundamental aspect of the argument. Extreme permissives cannot accept that some men and women have no discernible sexual attraction to their own sex. Taking refuge in words like "repression" and other misinterpreted psychological jargon, they succeed only in avoiding the issue. Similarly, anti-permissives are too quick to condemn any variation as a sign of decadent perversity. The true point at issue, the necessary goal of the revolution, is genuine freedom, the creation of a society in which heterosexuals, bisexuals and homosexuals can express themselves as they wish without fear, without running the risk of social condemnation. Extremists suggest that everyone must, in time, become bisexual, but this is nonsense and does much to strengthen the position of the detractors of permissiveness. Although it is true that we are, in a sense, all of us bisexual, it must never be forgotten that the majority are quite happy with a monosexual life. They are not the victims of dangerous repression and inhibition, but are balanced people leading satisfactory lives. It is with those who *are* repressed, whose sexual natures are unable to find satisfactory expression because of external prohibition, who should be the concern of the permissive revolution. When all is said and done, a unisexual world would be a dull one. Difference is the lifeblood of sexual attraction, like for like or among opposites. Just as we must learn to accept a multi-racial society, so must we establish, once and for all, the right of the individual to sleep with whom he likes. Considered in this light, the problem is really not so very great, the changes required to make its solution possible not so very radical.

In the meantime, the position of the bisexual becomes daily easier. We can be sure that he or she will not willingly let this new freedom and acceptance be taken from them. The process will be slow but the portents are more than favourable. Utopias are probably no more than chimeras, but the right of the individual to express himself sexually as and where he pleases is likely to become a fact.